DISSOLUTION TO EVOLUTION

NAVIGATING YOUR DIVORCE THROUGH THE CONSILIUM® PROCESS

Heidi-Rachel Webb and Julie Kunce Field

THE BRIEF PRESS/ LINCOLN, MASSACHUSETTS

ISBN (Print) 978-1-54392-311-7 (Ebook) 978-1-54392-312-4

Published by:
The Brief Press
Lincoln, MA 01773
www.consiliumdivorce.com

Contents

I dedicate this book to three men:

My father, J. Chester Webb - who was my mentor and model for "thinking outside the box", and taught me to believe in myself;

My college boyfriend- who by ending our relationship sensitized me to the trauma of ending a long-term relationship; and

My husband and soulmate, Andrew M. Singer, who has supported and nurtured me, believed in The Consilium® Process and encouraged me to disrupt the traditional divorce paradigm.

I further dedicate this book to one incredible woman, my mother, Gertrude M. Webb, who taught me that listening was more important than talking, and that where there is life, there is always hope.

I further dedicate this book to my children, Adam, Berkley and Francesca, who each in their own way inspire and humble me on a daily basis.

I also dedicate this book to my siblings, who learned with me from our parents that "you can disagree but you can't be disagreeable".

My parents live on in us in that, and so many other ways.

And to Julie Field, my co-author, esteemed colleague and treasured friend, who challenged me to write this book, agreed to co-write it with me and then travelled the road to turn it into a reality.

Thank you, and to continued adventures!

Additionally, I dedicate this book to the many hundreds of people who, at a most vulnerable time in their lives, placed their trust in me and in The Consilium® Process. I feel privileged to have played a small part in their lives, and awed and inspired by their journeys of growth and renewal.

Heidi-Rachel Webb

This book is dedicated to my husband, Stuart, a solid rock of support whose own journey as a writer has helped inspire mine. And to each of my remarkable children, Sam and Ellen, who continue to amaze me every day with their wit, energy, intelligence, and compassion. And, of course, to my parents Ken and Cecelia and to my brothers Kenny Joe and Jon and to my sister Amy; you have each taught me how to laugh, how to love, and how to continue on through the difficult times (note, that we are all fans of the Chicago Cubs. 'Nuf said).

And, finally, to Heidi. When I met Heidi in the summer of 1981, I knew I had found a friend, but I hadn't realized that I had found a trusted colleague who would travel a parallel path to mine in the law, and who would dedicate her career to creating a thoughtful, pioneering approach to dealing with family law issues. So, ultimately, this book is dedicated to you, Heidi, for having the persistence to share your vision with those who need help navigating the journey that is a family law case. Thank you, Heidi, for allowing me to be a part of your own journey, and I look forward to being part of more adventures to come!

Julie Kunce Field

ACKNOWLEDGEMENTS

This book would not have been possible without the help of many people along the way.

Special thanks go to my office staff, which is so much more than that to me! Gina Cronin is a paralegal extraordinaire, and Lisa Mancini who manages our office with grace and agility. Together they make seamless the integration between professional skill and personal warmth. Their creation of grids, formatting of this book, and endless attention to style and content just skim the surface as to why I feel grateful and blessed to have them as my colleagues.

My son, Adam Singer, is a talented writer in his own right. He is also a passionate learner, a media savvy millennial, and an eager collaborator. I feel honored to have had him be one of my first readers, grateful he willingly embraced this project and thankful for his relentless attention to editorial detail and the creative process.

I am also grateful to Lisa Paige, who is an extraordinary editor- (and a high school friend) - there's a theme here. Lisa read not only the words and sentences presented on the pages but she understood the book from the time of its inception, and along with her time and expertise willingly offered us her perspective and ideas for improved presentation. Her humor is unparalleled, and it was often the ingredient that took us from "impossible" to "ta-da". And I thank Heather Korostoff Murray a trusted friend, who early on embraced the Consilium ® Process, and then read my final manuscript draft and improved it in ways big and small.

PREFACE

I had just turned on the 11 o'clock news when a Marine's photo, identifying him by name flashed across the screen, taking my breath away. I recognized the young man, having known him as a three- year old child when his parents had divorced sixteen years earlier. At just nineteen years of age, he'd been killed in Fallujah, Iraq.

Tears filled my eyes. Immediately, I was transported back to the time when this now dead soldier, and his five-year-old sister were the much-loved fodder in their parents' contentious custody battle. At the time, I represented his mother. Zealously. I left no rock unturned in her quest to secure primary custody, which through our efforts she won.

Yet there was a price to this victory. The family would be divided in a way that would have huge implications on her children's sense of family moving forward. She was granted the right to move her young children from the town she'd lived in with her husband, to one about forty minutes from him. She remarried, as did the children's father. And they each had two more children. Periodically I heard from her and about the children- usually when things weren't going so well.

Fast forward sixteen years to the shattering news I'd just heard. I was shocked. I dialed my client's number and she answered her phone. I listened to her pain, learned when her son's body would be brought home, and where his funeral would be.

At the funeral, one of his high school teachers eulogized him saying that he'd joined the Marines because he wanted a family, as he felt like he'd never had one.

In that moment, I realized that no matter how well intended we'd been, the hours and efforts we'd expended had been misplaced. The system as I knew it was broken. The acrimony of the process had created distrust and alienation, contributing to a sense of brokenness that felt beyond repair to that young man.

I was changed at that funeral. And I vowed no longer to contribute to a system that destroyed families. Instead, I would work to create a process that would help families transition to a new form of family, in a way that left everyone whole, healthy and safe.

I began by researching the history of family law that has led us to the legal system we have today, as well as the growth and evolution in literature and research concerning human and psychological development. The Consilium® Process is the result of those facets having been examined under a different lens. It is my hope that this new paradigm contributes to the creation of healthier post-divorced families, not only for our generation, but also for all those that follow us.

INTRODUCTION

The beginning is a very good place to start ... or is it?

Fresh Tracks

Sometimes, when cross-country skiing, you have to step off the well-maintained trail and rest for a moment, breathe differently, and open your eyes more widely, to see an unexpected horizon of extraordinary beauty in the distance, a place that you had only dreamed of discovering. A pristine destination glowing with possibility.

I have had that experience, and not just on the ski mountain.

Once, I was an aggressive family law litigator, constantly in and out of court fighting passionately to get the best settlements I could for my clients. Over the more than twenty years I practiced this type of law, it was rare that I would remain in contact with a client after the divorce was finalized. If I did run into a client years later and ask how things were going, I often heard the disheartening news that the children still weren't sleeping through the night, or that their move into new careers or more independent lifestyles hadn't worked out as hoped.

These were not the outcomes I had labored so hard to procure for them.

Despite the consistency of these disillusioning reports, I was so close to the legal system that I could see no other approach. I was completely unaware that it was the construct of the divorce process itself that was failing my clients. Because I had bought into that construct, I too was part of the problem.

Sure, I had been trained in and directed many clients to the Collaborative Law approach, and yes, I knew of, practiced, and often recommended mediation. But somehow, in the rush to file the initial complaint and pursue the best possible settlement and custody arrangements, none of us— not my clients and surely not I—had stopped long enough to envision a better way through the entire process—a holistic approach that could radically alter the outcomes.

Simultaneously, I was growing disenchanted with my own lifestyle. Contrary to what we had all watched on "L.A. Law," there was really nothing all that glamorous about my high-stress litigator days when I could barely find time to go to one of my kids' school events, with the nanny was bringing up the children. With my schedule the way it was, there was no way our growing family could handle the addition of the one more child my husband and I both wanted to have. We decided together that we were fortunate enough to allow me a few years to step off the fast track and devote myself full-time to the family.

It was the best thing I ever could have done for my family, my career, and the people I serve as an attorney.

The transition started when I began to come to terms with new demands— the demands of the parents I met at my children's schools and activities, for advice on whether they should pursue divorce and, if so, how. My reputation as a successful and compassionate divorce attorney had literally preceded me onto my children's playgrounds. Finally, I realized the wisdom I had gained from watching so much misery could contribute to the development of a new approach to an increasingly demanding and distressing problem—the dissolution of the American family at an extremely high emotional cost for all involved.

I knew that it wasn't possible to save all marriages. That just didn't make sense. But I also recognized that something had to give in the way we were treating—or not—the individuals, including the children, who were suffering through divorce the way it was being handled.

I began meeting with a few potential clients, but I was reluctant to re-enter the practice of family law as I had lived it before. Additionally, I could not in good faith advise acquaintances and complete strangers without setting up responsible ethical parameters protecting both them and me. I found myself in a conundrum—neither wanting to go back into the courtroom nor wanting to abandon the deep wisdom I had gained over twenty-odd years of exposure to the trauma and challenges of untying the marriage knot.

In the course of my career, I had been exposed to the best practices and supports available to divorcing couples and their children. The problem, as I saw it, was that these services were disparate, dispersed, and often not prioritized. I recognized that families needed someone who could help them find where to turn to determine a) whether their marriage could be saved, b) what type of divorce process to pursue should the marriage be unsalvageable, and c) what their immediate and long-term priorities should be to ensure the mental and emotional health of all parties involved.

I wanted to see more compassion and conscious decision-making enter the process of ending a contract entered with such good intentions. I wanted to see families envisioning a way from destructive to constructive and into a future in which co-parenting and familial structures of a different sort could thrive. How amazing would it be, I thought, if instead of focusing only on the dissolution of a marriage, the parties could focus on the new beginning inherent in the transition? Why weren't we as a system approaching a divorce the way we approached so many other things in life, like an education plan or a career, with a plan for where we wanted to be five, ten years down the road?

Slowly, organically, and steadily, the basics of the Consilium® Process emerged, as I worked with a new and growing client base I had never expected I would have or had planned on serving. Instead of taking clients through the established steps of a divorce as learned in my family law classes and honed through years of practice, I began meeting with them as individuals, interviewing them more like a psychologist might, asking them what they saw as their *goals*. Concentrating on what they might like to see as a positive *outcome*.

As I broke the process down into its components, I began to recognize that there was a way to organize the divorce process entirely differently. By attending *from the start* to the psychosocial aspects, as well as to finances and property, my clients could begin to define where they wanted to go. I discovered that the best question I could ask a new client was where they would be happy seeing themselves in a few years, in that theoretical point in the future when I would run into them and ask them how they and their family were doing. All I really had to ask people was, "What do you want out of this process? Where do you want to be at the end of it?"

The answers were remarkable. Some had terrific ideas for new businesses or for going back to school to reach an entirely different career goal. Some had hopes to live in an entirely different paradigm they had never really defined before. Most had financial and relationship goals. All wanted the best for their children. Men and women alike, leavers and leaves, wanted to take new charge of their destinies and build better lives.

Today, after years of refining this new approach, of developing methodology and working with a wide variety of other professionals such as judges, financial planners, insurance providers, mental health practitioners, alternative therapists, and more, I don't often set foot in a courtroom. Instead, I help people discover that vista, the place miles down the untraveled road where they envision themselves and their families restructured, at peace, and thriving. Knowing where they want to be at the end makes it possible for them to journey down the road to get there.

Now, I feel good about my work. At the end of my day, I know that I have helped families avoid many of the pitfalls that I used to wade through with clients, armed for the worst confrontational battles imaginable. I share in their relief and yes, even joy, as they begin to surmount the challenges of familial restructuring, of untangling a marital knot in such a way that although the strands of the braid may no longer be intertwined, neither are they frayed beyond recognition.

In fact, many of my clients are now creating new tapestries from these same strands—tapestries rich with color and texture. Their lives are progressing in new ways, they are ready to forge new paths, and their children are thriving. The Consilium® Process works, and I'm eager to share it with you.

The Consilium® 7-step Process includes:

1. Interview and Intake: What to Expect
2. Assessment and Envisioning a Future
3. Creating a Parallel Path
4. Choosing the Right Divorce Process
5. Finding Appropriate Counsel and Professional Supports
6. Staying on Track
7. Outcomes

We have written this book with case studies which incorporate and illustrate the elements of the Consilium® Process. At the end of the book, we've provided a workbook for you to use as a guide for your own process.

It is our hope that the case studies will provide perspective on a variety of situations, and that one or a combination of them will resonate with you and help you as you journey forward in the restructuring of your own life and that of your family.

In our work with individual clients we create detailed legal, financial, and social/emotional plans for them and their attorneys. If you would like to work with us to create your own individualized plan, you can contact us at info@consiliumdivorce.com.

TWO JOURNEYS

Imagine if you were about to embark on a journey to Italy. You woke up one morning and decided to pack your bags and get on a plane. You don't speak the language, but you decide to take things as they come.

Once you get there, you need to find a hotel room. It may be high-priced or low-priced depending on what's available and how much your budget is. The one you like may or may not be available.

You'll need to eat that evening. You may or may not find a reservation at a restaurant that you like. Maybe you think strolling around a neighborhood reading menus in the windows of restaurants sound good--until you are so hungry you just pick one out of desperation.

The next day, you decide you want to see some sights. You didn't buy any tickets ahead of time, so you may not be able to see popular destinations like the Vatican and you definitely won't be able to see da Vinci's "Last Supper." You may or may not be able to find a guide with vast experience. You could be wandering around without even so much as a map of the city or a book detailing the history and architectural details.

Now, imagine if you had decided two months earlier that you would like to visit Italy. You procured a map of Rome, Florence, and Milan, and circled the sights that are most interesting to you. You went online and bought the tickets for the most popular sights to ensure entry. You secured a hotel in the location and budget of your choosing. This hotel also has all the amenities you require when you stay away from home. You made reservations at restaurants that looked appealing to you. You hired a guide to take you around to places that you are particularly interested in. Since he has lived there all his life and is steeped in the history, culture and language of his homeland, he can take you to places you might not otherwise have been able to learn about.

Finally, imagine the differences in these two journeys. In the first, you may have a great time. You might stay in a place that you like, eat at sweet local restaurants, see the sights you are interested in. However, it is all left to chance. The second journey gives you your best chance of having an amazing trip, and still allows for flexibility when you choose.

The divorce process can also look like either of the above journeys. You can jump blindly and hope for the best, or you can slow down, plan, and create the best itinerary for moving forward.

Lawyers are trained to analyze fact patterns and look for solutions that can be achieved within the bounds of the law. Psychologists are also trained to listen and look for patterns, but those with emotional and psychological underpinnings that might account for behaviors that, when understood, might help people change. When helping those confronting divorce, both kinds of listening are helpful; however, until now, those two disparate perspectives have not been taught together in any coordinated manner. Having a background in both perspectives, it became clear to me that the unnatural divisions in our schooling were counterproductive for our clients. If we want to help people resolve their financial and contractual obligations under the law, and heal their emotional wounds and hurts, best practices dictate that we merge those practices to navigate that chasm.

I started asking different questions—ones lawyers didn't typically ask. In fact, I started asking questions lawyers often shy away from, as they aren't based on a legal premise and don't seem to directly address issues that lead to either a settlement or positioning for Court. But what if these questions *do* help reach a settlement or lead to positioning for court? Questions like:

- "Where do you hope to be in ten years? In five years? In three years?"
- "If we were having this conversation in three years, what would have to have happened for you to feel satisfied about this process?"
- "Could you tell me what your husband/wife would tell me if he/she were sitting here right now? Can you tell me about your children?"

These questions differ from typical questions about assets and debt, income and expenses. Those questions are of course also important, but we reach them along different paths. Consilium® questions are not intended to assess and assign blame, but rather to optimize the restructuring of a family. It should be noted that if abuse or addictions are issues of concern, and they have not yet been acknowledged or dealt with, this process cannot be employed until other appropriate interventions are in place. However, in the vast majority of cases, parents can and do wish to co-parent after divorce. And this process has also proven to be helpful as part of a process during recovery or other therapeutic interventions.

Parents typically want to uncouple but they do not want to "un-parent." When the wounds created through the divorce are worse than those created during the marriage, the system is broken. If every time patients went to the hospital, they came out sicker than when they went in, they would stop going. However, unlike choices we make about our voluntary medical care, the State has a voice in a marriage (hence also in a divorce), and therefore, married people are forced to involve the State in the dissolution of their marriages. The first step in fixing this problem is recognizing that as participants in this structure we could do better.

As lawyers we are trained in the art of language. Word choice matters. From the very first Consilium® interview, we actively shift traditional language. Instead of talking about divorce, we talk about restructuring families, and instead of talking about custody, we talk about co-parenting. The walls we build are undulating; we recognize the importance of boundaries, but also the importance of creating "give and take."

We aim to build knowledge and competence when we talk about money and finance. We help clients create working budgets, not simply financial statements for filing in Court. We help clients think through their cost of living not only for today, but also into the future for the education of their children and perhaps themselves, and into retirement. We help our clients understand business valuations and real estate appraisals. They become educated about both content and context. When appropriate we work with financial analysts and help our clients hire investment managers.

As the Consilium® Process is geared to helping clients frame the restructuring of their lives and those of their families, and part of that process involves hiring lawyers and/or mediators, we also help clients understand how best to navigate legal terrain, and how to interview and hire appropriate lawyers. In order for you to do that, we will share how we did this in each of the cases that follow, which we have chosen as illustrative, and then direct you through a series of grids in the Appendices so that you are equipped to answer questions for yourself, interview multiple lawyers, and better understand how each one would approach helping you restructure your family.

Key elements for successful family restructuring

- Starting the process with a framework: legal, financial, emotional, and personal goal planning.

- Hiring the right counsel that is not based simply on reputation or word of mouth, but rather who is truly a match for your personal situation and the process or processes you decide to pursue.

- Pre-planning what aspects of your divorce might be best suited to which process (perhaps litigating one portion and mediating or arbitrating another) and "custom fitting" your case accordingly.

- Knowing the intricacies of finances not only for today, but also for three, five, or fifteen years from now.

- Creating an atmosphere where you and your children are well cared for emotionally throughout the process.

- Establishing attainable goals for your new life.

PART II: CASE STUDIES

TRAVELING JOURNEY # 1

Sarah and Joe - Failing to slow down

It's better to do the right thing slowly than the wrong thing quickly

- Peter Turla

First meeting

Sarah was in a rush when she arrived fifteen minutes late for her initial consultation with me. She was hurried in her speech and spent the first five minutes of our time checking her messages on her phone.

Sarah's intake sheet was sparse--she reported that she had been married to Joseph for fifteen years, that she is thirty-eight years old, Joseph is forty, and that they have two children, Emma (10) and Greg (8).

She reported that she hadn't worked outside of the home since Emma was eighteen months old. Sarah had trained as an art teacher, but would have to renew her license before she could be considered for a new job. Joseph worked as an engineer for a local software start-up, and handled all their money. Sarah was not clear on how much money he made, or what the family budget was. Lastly, she said that they lived in a quiet suburb in a nice home, which they had bought for a "pretty low price, given the market" in 2009. The only other information included on the intake form was her statement at the bottom, in all capital letters: "I NEED TO FILE FOR A DIVORCE NOW!!!!!!!!!!!!!!!!!!!!" (*emphases hers.*)

I tried to help Sarah relax a bit, and tell me why she felt like she was in such a rush to get a divorce. Was there violence? No, never. Was there a concern about the children around Joseph for any reason? "No, of course not," was her answer. Was there an affair going on? Something that would have led Sarah to feel such urgency? "Not really." She told me that it was just time. Things hadn't been working for a few years, and she was tired of the same old routine and feeling like unpaid help. She saw two of her close friends get divorces, and thought they had "made out okay" in regard to alimony and child support. Sarah was sure she'd be fine, too.

Despite my efforts to slow her down, Sarah remained rushed in how she spoke, as if she couldn't take the time to listen to the advice she had come to me for.

She told me that she had made this appointment between a lunch date with a friend and picking up her kids from school, and that she needed to leave in half an hour or she would be late (again) to get the kids. I described the process that I use with my clients: **planning**, thinking about the future, envisioning life after divorce, and learning what the different divorce processes entail. I told her that I would need more time with her, and more basic information to get started on that **planning** process. I explained that filing without **planning** was **planning** to fail. Filing in a rush would not give her the best options for resolving her divorce, or create an effective post-divorce restructuring of her family.

Throughout our conversation, she kept glancing at her phone. When I asked her what she was doing, she said she had to keep an eye on the time. I suggested that we set up another appointment, and that she come back when she had more time to focus on the divorce planning process. She agreed to call back that afternoon and set up another appointment for the next week.

I never heard back from Sarah until....

Second meeting

Nine months later, I got a call from an attorney I know well. He told me that he was calling with Sarah's permission because he had filed Sarah's divorce case nine months previously – *the day after* she had met with me. Sarah had asked him to call me because she had remembered our conversation about planning, and she was ready to start planning with me now if I was still able to work with her. I told him I would be happy to talk with him about her if she signed a release.

Sarah came in with her attorney a couple of weeks later. I asked him for a basic update of their divorce process. He told me that Sarah had signed a final agreement in her divorce. She had agreed to maintenance of $500 per month for two years, which I thought was well below the amount she should have gotten under the statute. Her attorney agreed, but told me that Sarah had insisted on entering into the agreement against his advice, because she "just wanted out," and was exhausted by the legal process.

The children were spending half of their time with their father, who had remained in the marital home. Sarah had agreed to allow Joseph a year to refinance the house to buy out her share.

Sarah was struggling financially, and was trying to get back to work as an art teacher. She needed to take additional classes to update her license, had moved twice (since moving out of their family home), and wasn't sure where all of her documentation for her teaching certification was. She wanted to work in a weekend arts program to make more money, but that would cut into the time she could spend with her children.

In short, she was a mess, and hoped that I could help her fix things now.

I spoke candidly to Sarah and to her attorney. After an agreement is signed and accepted by the court, there isn't a lot that can be done to change alimony or the terms of a property buy-out. Some things could be done to modify child support and parenting time, but even those options were limited. Although I listened carefully and with a compassionate ear, I was sad to see that Sarah had been in such a hurry to get divorced that she hadn't thought about what the rest of her life would really be like.

Outcomes

Had Sarah slowed herself down, and given more thought to how she wanted her life to be post-divorce, she would likely have ended up better off.

What went wrong? It seemed that just about everything had!

Sarah was so certain that she wanted to get divorced that she'd jumped into the deep end without knowing how to swim. She found herself acting rashly instead of with foresight. It's also likely that her actions incited Joseph, triggering his least generous instincts. He probably wasn't thinking holistically or long-term. His primary concern was simply to protect himself.

What could have been done differently?

Giving Sarah supports as she moved into the divorce process could have slowed her down long enough to plan thoughtfully. She could have anticipated the requirements of reinstating her teaching licensure, how long it would take, and how much it would cost, to make that happen. With that knowledge, Sarah could have worked those costs and that timeframe into her divorce settlement agreement.

Depending upon the complexities of her re-licensing, Sarah might have been able to start working as a teacher again prior to filing for divorce, or at least begin the process of looking for a job. Having reliable income would certainly have helped her create a financial buffer as she adjusted to post-divorce life.

No mention was made of her husband's reaction to her having filed a divorce complaint. If he felt angry and betrayed, his response may well have been vindictive, or at least unyielding. If instead she had discussed with him her reasons for wanting to restructure their family, she might have found that he too was unhappy, and that together they could agree to thoughtfully attend to the needs of their children, and optimize the outcomes of everyone involved.

If Sarah had given forethought to her actions, she could have anticipated the needs of their children and identified and/or consulted with therapists, so that the children would have had a support-network during their parents' divorce.

Having a full knowledge of their finances would have allowed Sarah to analyze what elements of her lifestyle would need to change post divorce. Perhaps instead of needing to move twice, she could have planned and budgeted realistically for her post-divorce circumstances. Working with a mortgage broker in advance of moving out of her first family home would have armed her with knowledge as to what she would need to establish credit and income to qualify for a mortgage on her own. Sarah could have addressed issues of debt or bad credit that might put her financial house in disarray before they *became* issues.

Furthermore, working with her own therapist and/or a couples' therapist could have helped Sarah (and Joseph) understand how their marriage had gone wrong, so that they could avoid repeating those same patterns with future partners.

Working with a Consilium® Divorce Consultant would have given Sarah the knowledge she needed to streamline her decisions, hire appropriate legal counsel, consider her children's future and happiness, and thoughtfully restructure her family with Joseph.

Planning for a divorce, and establishing appropriate supports makes all the difference. Instead of ending up with a "broken" family, the couple can create a "restructured" one, which will benefit everyone much more in the long run.

Through this book and workbook, we will guide you through the Consilium® process, so that you can avoid the pitfalls Sarah encountered.

TRAVELING JOURNEY # 2

Marguerite and Alex — Slowing things down

As Carl Honore said <u>In Praise of Slow,</u> the slow philosophy is not about doing everything in tortoise mode. It's less about the speed and more about investing the right amount of time and attention in the problem so you solve it.

When Marguerite walked into my office, the first thing she told me was that she felt trapped. She couldn't see options for herself other than remaining in her unhappy marriage, yet she couldn't imagine remaining in it either.

She made plans in her mind, but couldn't bring herself to act on any of them. In part, her paralysis was born out of fear that her plans would result in chaos and unhappiness for her children, and in part she didn't think her husband, Alex, would be able to survive on his own.

As I began to explore with her the reasons for her feelings, she told me that she regarded Alex as a "highly functioning" alcoholic, but that she absolutely couldn't trust him alone with their children. She couldn't imagine sharing custody with him, or relying on him to drive them anywhere.

When I asked Marguerite if she ever left the children alone with Alex (they were at the time nine, eight and five years old), she responded by telling me that she had recently gone to a friend's wedding in Oregon, and hired a babysitter to be with them while she was away, as she couldn't envision her husband taking care of them on his own for an entire weekend. When she arrived home, she found the babysitter gone, her husband in bed with a bottle of vodka, and the children fending for themselves. She was grateful no one had been hurt, but it cemented her belief that he was incapable of being alone with the children for a few days at a stretch.

Marguerite told me further that there had been numerous occasions when she had come home to find Alex so drunk that she would leave with the children and go to a hotel, telling the children it was a fun adventure of one sort or another. This behavior suggested that Alex was less functional than Marguerite wished to believe. True, alcoholism is a disease, but if it is to be treated, the first steps must come from the alcoholic. Marguerite had grown tired of the lies and machinations she had to orchestrate in order to maintain some semblance of normalcy for their kids, and she suspected that at least their oldest daughter recognized all was not well at home. Marguerite couldn't enable his alcoholism any longer.

Finances

During our initial meeting, Marguerite told me that she had left household financial management to her husband. By the end of our conversation, she realized that understanding the income and expenses of their lifestyle would be her first step to making a real plan as to how she could move forward. Making a concrete financial plan is necessary for you, too. It is the first critical step you need to make, in order to gain clarity and understanding about what changes you may or may not need to make in order to take your next steps forward. Without having the numbers in front of you, your ideas and dreams will remain just that.

Special supports for special cases

Marguerite had enormous compassion for Alex. She saw him as a deeply wounded person, and worried that without her, he would self-destruct and be unable to cope. In addition, she wasn't at all certain that divorce was what she wanted. We talked about the possibility of a therapeutic intervention, which would culminate in an alcohol rehab program for Alex. She also discussed what would have to happen for her to want to stay in their marriage: what Alex would need to do for her to stay and what she would need to do if she decided to leave. We then identified her emotional supports, as well as Alex's. It was clear that if Marguerite were ever to feel comfortable enough to leave Alex, she would first need to know that he had adequate emotional supports.

If Marguerite were going to attempt an intervention, or convince Alex that he needed to go to rehab in an attempt to save their marriage, if not for his own health and future, Marguerite needed to identify who would be on her "team." She decided that the first person she needed was Alex's sister, and that the first thing she would need to do was tell her about his drinking. She would also need to find a time when Alex was sober to talk to him about his drinking, its impact on their family, and how necessary it was that he deal with it in order for her to stay in their marriage.

We also talked about creating a timeline so that she could have benchmarks she valued in terms of making progress in their marriage, and thereby decide whether to divorce or restructure it. Marguerite decided that having a three-year timeline would create a "bright line in the sand" for her. It would give her time to try to help Alex conquer his demons that were causing and being exacerbated by his drinking, and time for her to get back into the workforce. It would give her time to evaluate where each of their children were educationally and emotionally, and plan and provide any necessary supports to ease the transitions they would inevitably encounter if she decided her only alternative was to divorce and restructure their family.

In any situation involving addiction, it's *especially* important to identify emotional supports and timelines for both parties—and especially for the children.

Legal approaches

Despite having given herself a fairly long time-line, Marguerite also wanted to learn about different ways to divorce. Although it seemed a bit premature to begin to interview lawyers and/or mediators to hire, it wasn't too early to begin to understand the various processes, and also to calculate a likely range of child support, spousal support and a division of marital assets. As always, creating a realistic financial picture will allow for realistic planning.

The workbook section of this book contains an income and expense grid for you to fill out. This will help you frame your current financial picture, and will allow you to start thinking about how to structure a financial model for your restructured family.

The workbook will also help you identify educational and mental health support needs for you and your family.

ONE JUDGE'S PERSPECTIVE.

I have worked on family law cases for over thirty years, first as a law student intern in the chilly courtrooms of Chicago, later as an attorney for millionaire entrepreneurs, then as a law professor overseeing law students in clinics representing poor clients who were fighting for custody and who were often trying to escape from domestic violence, and more recently, as a court-appointed family law mediator. As an attorney, I've worked in countless courtrooms in five different states. And I've been a judge for six years where I've seen all kinds of people come to court looking for clarity in their family law case. It has been both my privilege, and my burden, to help people at what is often the most significant event in their lives, and what is usually the only time that they have contact with the court system. I work hard to make that contact be as positive as it can be under the circumstances, but better planning and preparation on the part of the people who are in court seeking a divorce can make it much easier both during and after the process.

In all of those experiences, I have seen many things that are common with people who are going through the challenge of a family law case. First, many people are still reeling from the significant change that is happening in their lives. Many people never expected it or, if they did see it coming well before they filed in court, they still are mourning the loss of what was, and what could have been. Some people show that reaction to change and loss as anger and blame, others as sadness, still others as resignation, and some as optimism and hope for the future. Second, I have learned that openness, honesty, and kindness, both as an attorney representing people at this difficult time in their lives, and as a judge who sees people in what is one of the worst times of their lives, can provide a pathway to a positive outcome. Third, I know that at least some of my colleagues – lawyers and judges – are not always able to individualize the parties or the cases and honor the circumstances that have brought this family before a court. And, in addition to all of those considerations, what I frequently find is that I have too little information, with too much extraneous distraction, to make the best decision for this family. But I, and my thoughtful colleagues, try to do the best with what we have. When you are involved in a family law case in front of a judge, particularly when you are looking to the judge to make significant decisions about your finances and parenting, you can benefit from preparation, focus, and dealing with the personal challenges with integrity and grace, even when circumstances make it hard to do that.

You might hear people remind you that you and your spouse will continue to be parents even after the divorce. How you treat each other, and your children, will guide their lives, and their own future relationships. Unless you have concerns about domestic violence or child abuse and are driven by a priority of safety, work hard not to disparage the other parent with the children. Knowing that children benefit from an expansion of love from many people – each parent, grandparents, step-family members – it can be helpful to keep in mind that spending time with those people and other safe family members is going to help them in the long run. Speaking badly about the other parent when they are safe but perhaps not perfect may backfire and end up turning your children against you.

First as a mediator and now as a judge, I guide people to be three things: focused, productive, and professional. What I mean by that is that divorcing parties need to keep their focus on what the long-term goals are, to be productive in seeking outcomes that they can live with, and to be professional in addressing the business of the dissolution of the partnership that is their marriage. People who are focused, productive, and professional throughout the entirety of the process generally fare better in both the process and in the long run. While it is not always easy to be each of those three things, the more focused, productive, and professional you can be not just in court hearings but throughout the process, the better the outcome will be for you and the more satisfaction you will have, even when things are really, really hard. If you keep "focused, productive, and professional" as your mantra in court or in related meetings, I believe you will be more in control of yourself, and your reactions to unexpected surprises that might surface as you move through the court and into your post-divorce life. The tools of the Consilium® Process are designed to help you keep focused, productive, and professional. The Consilium® Process is itself an innovation that can help people navigate the challenges of divorce and custody cases with grace and dignity.

As I said, it is often the case that people come to divorce without planning or thought about what they want or need, or what their long-term goals are for their future and the future of their children. Without such thoughtful planning and preparation for the future, divorcing parties are likely to be unhappy both with the process and the outcome. It is easy in a divorce case to be carried along by the heat of the moment – and to have your actions governed by anger or revenge – even where that is out of character for you in the rest of your life.

The Consilium® Process helps you focus by prioritizing what is important, by envisioning and setting attainable goals, by knowing the steps you need to take to determine the best process for you by considering who you are, who your spouse is, and what your children need. The tools of the Consilium® Process have been designed through years of refinement with all types of individual clients to help you take the steps that you need to take to reach those long-term, post-divorce goals. As you can see from all of the information that is available about divorce and the legal process of divorce, it can be easy to lose track of what you need to do, how you need to do it, and how to understand and then select the best process for your individual situation. With the guidance of the Consilium® Process, you will be able to be productive and minimize the overall financial and emotional cost of your divorce.

As an attorney and mediator, I would tell my family law clients then the same thing that I tell the parties who are in front of me in court now on family law cases– even when divorce is the right thing, it is still a hard thing. The Consilium® Process can make that hard thing a little easier, and a lot more focused, productive, and professional, and with better outcomes for you, your spouse, and your children.

Honorable Julie Kunce Field

PART III: GIVING CONTEXT TO PROCESS

The following case studies are intended to help you understand the various processes available for a marital dissolution. They will illustrate why, how, and when mediation, litigation, collaborative law, and hybrid processes are best employed. Lesser utilized options will also be identified and discussed.

LITIGATION "LITE"©

"If I am not for others, what am I?" - Rabbi Hillel

Natasha and Drew

Initial consult

When I first met with Natasha, she was reeling with raw emotion. Her life seemed to be unraveling before her eyes and she told me that she hadn't anticipated any of it. She had thought that her life was going along quite comfortably. She and her husband of nine years had two young boys, five and seven years old. The older boy, Aidan, was on the autism spectrum, and Natasha said that although he was progressing well and had been mainstreamed into a public school, raising him was trying. She was full of pride when she told me how very bright Aidan was, and how focused he was on making social gains. She described her younger son, Brendan, as a typical learner and a generally happy kid, although at times he understandably found his brother difficult to get along with.

It was clear from the moment Natasha walked into my office that she was depleted and exhausted. It didn't take long for me to see Natasha as a "giver"—so much so in fact that it was hard for her to make sure her own needs and desires were being met. And she was steadfast about wanting to put her children's needs first. I saw an inner strength in Natasha; despite her disappointment and anger, I knew she would put her children's interests, and those of her restructured family, ahead of her own. What Natasha would need was someone who would be her ally and her advocate. Her voice needed to be heard. But first, she had to find it.

History

Natasha told me that she and her husband, Drew, had met their first year out of college, when they were both working as forest rangers in the National Park system. They both had a great love of the outdoors; their early years together had been spent hiking and camping all over the United States. However, after they got married, and before they had children, Drew decided that he wanted to pursue a more conventional career path that would enable him to support their family more easily.

Drew's undergraduate degree was in economics, and in college he had considered working in the financial world. He explored those possibilities by beginning a job as a stockbroker, based in Colorado. Natasha enjoyed living there, and described that phase of their marriage as extremely happy. Soon, Aidan was born, and Brendan followed shortly afterward.

Aidan's development became a concern, and Natasha devoted a great deal of time to getting him the help he needed. Drew's hours were long, and Natasha's focus shifted more and more to Aidan's needs, as well as the more typical needs of Brendan.

We started working together in the fall. The previous May, Drew had told Natasha he had an offer to move up with the company, but that it would entail a move to Boston. Natasha's extended family was in Maine, and she liked the idea of being closer to them. She also knew that the medical and educational opportunities in Boston could be a great asset for Aidan.

By June, they had packed up their house and moved to an apartment just outside of Boston. Having made a handsome profit on the sale of their Colorado home, coupled with the fact that Drew's employer had given them $25,000 toward the down-payment on their new home, Natasha was game to begin searching for a house.

However, in July, Drew told her—to her great astonishment—that he wasn't happy and wanted to separate. He suggested that he move into another apartment in the same complex where they were renting, a place that Natasha believed was only a temporary arrangement during the house search. Despite having her expectations upended, Natasha remained hopeful. She rationalized that this two-apartment arrangement would make things simpler for Aidan and Brendan, and give Drew time to think things over. She saw his move as a temporary separation, and hoped that before long he'd decide to move back in with her and the boys.

Over the course of the next month, Natasha noticed that a particular car (not Drew's) was frequenting the parking area near her husband's apartment, and she grew suspicious. When she confronted Drew, he told her that he was in love with a colleague and wanted a divorce.

Naturally, Natasha felt betrayed, hurt and overwhelmed. She couldn't imagine how she was going to raise her boys without Drew's support, and feared she'd never be able to leave the rented apartment she was in with Aidan and Brendan and live in the home she'd envisioned buying with Drew.

First steps

Natasha is a quiet woman by nature, and not comfortable reaching out for help. Her exhaustion was palpable. The combination of Drew's affair and their cross-country move had worn her out. She was without a local support system, and felt incredibly vulnerable.

Natasha recognized that by not seeking a cooperative arrangement with her husband, she would stand to lose his support of their children; her long game demanded that he be on board to help their children. She also knew her children needed him in their lives. She began to see the benefits (not only to her, but also to the children) of her beginning therapy. Despite Natasha's anger and frustration, she could own her part in the dissolution of their relationship, which she could address in therapy, both for resolution and to avoid repeating the pattern.

Having had the courage to seek help from us, Natasha was developing the ability to find additional counseling. Although Natasha told me it wasn't in her nature to want to "do therapy," she did feel like it could be helpful.

Natasha's future

Natasha and I talked about where she wanted to be in three, five, and ten years, and began to construct a path to help her get there. By focusing on her own growth, she could begin to see a way through a situation that had previously felt chaotic and unwieldy. She could start to see her divorce as part of her experience, not as something that would forever define who she is.

Natasha needed to map out a legal plan but she also needed to structure a personal plan so that she could rediscover the woman she had been before she met Drew. Consumed as she was with Aidan and Brendan, she needed to create supports for herself and begin to re-envision her future.

Before jumping right into legal action, it was critical for Natasha to figure out where she would live, what her budget would be, and what school systems would be suitable for Aidan and Brendan. She also needed to plan for her own future and growth. Alimony and child support would be forthcoming. The larger question was how she could make the best long-term use of the alimony that she'd receive for somewhere in the vicinity of six to seven years. What I didn't want Natasha to do was jump into legal action without first considering critical pieces of her own life. If she jumped first and thought later, she might find herself without the latitude she'd need to implement the life she wanted to create.

Natasha told me that she'd always wanted to be a librarian. As an undergraduate, she'd been an English literature major. She'd never pursued becoming a librarian because, like many "stay at home moms," once she had children, her energies were directed toward them and not toward herself or her career. However, by thinking ahead six or seven years to a time when the boys would be 13 and 15 years old, she could begin to think about how their day-to-day needs would be less demanding, and how she might have the bandwidth and desire to work.

As preparation for that time, Natasha began to look at graduate programs in library science and found two programs she liked in the Boston area. Both offered part-time options. Realizing that she could stretch a two-year program into four years gave her the confidence to apply to both programs.

By starting with herself, Natasha began to refocus her energy into a positive direction. Alongside her divorce, she could create her own parallel path of growth. She could envision and appreciate the difference an advanced degree would make in her future. Even if she didn't start her new career immediately upon finishing her program, she would eventually be able to settle into the career she'd always wanted to have.

By making this plan, Natasha could build her continuing education into a form of spousal support. With the likely award of six to seven years of alimony, she now saw how to use her spousal support wisely, so that when it discontinued, between the child support she would receive from Drew and her own income as a librarian, her lifestyle would continue without much disruption.

Together, we were able to craft the beginning terms of a Divorce Agreement that would incorporate not only Natasha's immediate concerns but also those of her future goals and dreams. She now saw that though the divorce was not her choice, she could be the agent of her own future, which empowered her to be creative and positive.

The children

Natasha's innate generosity led to a conversation about the positives Drew brought to Aidan and Brendan, and how she wanted him to remain an important presence in their lives. Natasha understood how important it would be for Drew not to feel marginalized as a parent, and to be invested in the upbringing of his sons. It would also be likely to engender more generosity from Drew to Natasha if he didn't feel sidelined. Shared custody would be important for Aidan and Brendan, and Natasha would benefit individually as it would also be a great source of support in terms of juggling her school schedule, and during the inevitable twists and turns of their children's development. Thus, even despite the emotional turmoil of marital infidelity, with careful forethought, Natasha concluded she and Drew could effectively co-parent, and they and their children would benefit.

Determining the right legal process

Although Drew and Natasha were being cordial to one another, Natasha naturally felt deeply wounded. She told me that she didn't have "the stomach" to sit in the same room with Drew to negotiate her future, but that she wanted to be fair, and eventually, amicable. She wanted some clarity around her immediate financial needs, and time to sift through her priorities so that she could create a strategic financial plan for herself. And in the hopes that she and Drew would be able to co-parent effectively, she wanted to maintain whatever goodwill she still felt toward him.

In light of Natasha's legal and personal needs, I didn't feel that either mediation or Collaborative Law would serve her well. She needed some immediate definition around finances, and she needed an advocate.

By the same token, I knew that with time she would grow stronger, and she wanted to preserve the best of her shared history with Drew. Hiring a lawyer who would run into Court "with guns a-'blazin'" wouldn't serve her well in the long run. Natasha needed someone who could use the Court process on an as-needed basis; someone who could negotiate for her now; someone who would make room for her to find her own voice; and someone who would help her articulate her own needs. She needed what I call "litigation-lite." She also needed to be coached so that she could appeal to Drew's best self, to lessen the likelihood of his hiring someone who would work at cross-purposes with her goals and those of their restructured family.

Individual goals

Since we were working with only one party, and addressing her short and long-term goals, I asked Natasha to write out both her goals, and what she believed Drew's were. By anticipating Drew's goals as well, she would be better equipped to think more fully about the consequences of her own objectives.

Natasha's goals

- Gain clarity about her spousal and child support
- Build a long-term financial plan
- Go back to school and establish her own career

- Create a good working Co-Parent relationship with Drew
- Nurture a deep and satisfying relationship with both of her children
- Have Aidan and Brendan grow up to be secure and independent adults
- Begin therapy to gain perspective on her marriage and herself
- Eventually develop a new and trusting relationship with a partner.

Natasha's imagined goals of Drew

- Be divorced as quickly as possible without contentiousness
- Pay as little support to Natasha as possible
- Protect his finances and future earnings
- Prevent Natasha from being angry at him
- Avoid hurting Natasha more than he already has
- Support Aidan and Brendan
- Buy a house of his own
- Co-Parent with Natasha
- Be unencumbered by the boys while still having them in his life
- Have a relationship with Aidan and Brendan
- Have Aidan and Brendan grow up to be secure and independent adults, while avoiding worry about Aidan's future

Considering another model for Litigation "Lite"

Molly and John

Initial Meeting

Molly was tentative as she approached my door. I was surprised by her appearance. Her white hair was neatly cropped, almost severely so. She wore a crisply ironed Peter Pan collared shirt, a pink cashmere sweater, a navy blue pleated skirt and penny loafers that were in good condition but looked like they were from the 1960's. She was prim and proper and chose her words carefully.

In her mid-70s, Molly was in the throes of reevaluating her marriage. She was struggling to understand the spoken and unspoken contracts she had made with her husband, and whether, if and why she wanted to stay in her marriage. She was seeing me at the urging of her therapist as she'd been talking to her about divorce for many years, but didn't really have any idea what the reality of that path would look like for her.

In our first conversation, Molly told me that although she wouldn't say she loved John, they had two children and forty-five years of married life behind them. He also had Stage Two cancer and despite the anger she felt toward him, she also felt loyalty if not affection. Much as she felt disconnected from John, she didn't like the idea of living alone, having long drawn out separation and/or divorce negotiations with him while he was sick, and risking the children feeling that she was heartless to divorce their father at this point in his life, when he was gravely ill.

From our Intake Form, I already knew her age, that she had been married for just over forty-five years, and that she and her husband had survived financial difficulties. They had raised their children in a wealthy Boston suburb, and were now living in a modest home in a working-class town. Her husband had received a large inheritance, but now none of it was left.

Why, *now*, had she sought out my services? She told me she was just on a fact- gathering mission. What would her life look like if she were to pursue a divorce? Could she afford a divorce? Would she be able to keep her house and maintain her lifestyle? Each of those concerns was punctuated by a story about how unhappy she was, how much her husband drank and how controlling he was. She told me that for many years, they'd been living parallel lives--hers focused primarily around the church and his focused primarily around a group of retired friends. Although it was true that she was unhappily married, more than a divorce, she was looking for leverage within their marriage. She wanted to understand their finances and she craved more independence, even in her home. She wanted to be able to stand up for herself and tell her husband that she knew her rights, and that if things didn't change, she was prepared to act to exact what she knew she was entitled to.

Finances and personalities

Molly told me that John had made some bad investment decisions. She also shared that she didn't know much about what had happened, as he was very "private" about anything having to do with money. As we talked more, it seemed to me that "secretive" would have been a more accurate word. Molly knew as little about their household money as she did about their larger investment picture. She had always received an "allowance" from John, enough to buy groceries and purchase herself clothing from time to time.

Molly struck me as someone who was frozen in time; everything from her style of dress to her style of speech screamed 1950's. John and Molly had grown up in privileged households, attended prep schools and elite colleges, but none of that translated into their ability to have a partnership of mutual respect, nor could she remember a time when it ever had.

According to Molly, John was very proud. Although he'd been unemployed for the past fifteen years, he refused to ask friends or family for help of any kind. He arranged his days around socializing--at a coffee shop, with his bicycling group, and at his social club. He had begun to drink, and his addiction was taking a toll on his body. At a recent visit to the doctor, following a fall while inebriated, his doctor had told him he had to stop drinking. Unfortunately, John ignored this advice. Because John did not typically welcome Molly's presence at his medical appointments, she didn't have a true understanding of his cancer prognosis.

As we talked more, Molly's fear of John became apparent. His verbal abuse was constant, and when I asked her if she feared for her physical safety, she burst into tears. She told me that a few years ago John had grabbed her by the neck and threatened to kill her. She attributed his behavior to stress, and it was at that point she insisted that in order to contain their living expenses, they needed to sell their house and downsize. Before she knew it, John came home telling her he'd put an offer in on a house in a community about an hour from where they were then living. Molly was shocked.

Molly had taken two strong stances in her marriage: (1) by saying they needed to move, and (2) that she would not simply be "transplanted" by John. After doing that, they were then able to negotiate, and with the assistance of a loan from Molly's mother, they purchased a new home much closer to their old one.

Since they moved (two years before she sought my counsel), they were living parallel lives. They slept in separate bedrooms and conducted their lives independently of one another. She had her own car and she drove to see friends and her mother, to church, and for shopping. They no longer shared meals, and communicated only in their bi-weekly marital counseling session.

Molly and John had been seeing the same marriage counselor for more than fifteen years. When I later spoke with their counselor, he described himself as the dialysis machine of their marriage, and said Molly was now questioning the wisdom of sustaining the marriage. She was tired of living in an oppressive household, and of living with someone who clearly did not want her input into his life.

To divorce or not to divorce

Molly concluded that if the power imbalance in her marriage could be altered, and she could feel some self-respect, she might be able to stay in her marriage. Knowing she had more control over her own choices, both financial and personal, would give her new confidence and agency. Once she knew fact from fiction, John's threats wouldn't have the same impact on her, and his words would no longer intimidate her. Knowing that if John faltered she would have the strength of the law behind her gave Molly a sense of confidence and strength. Even her body language spoke to that: her backbone straightened and her shoulders relaxed.

We talked about the difference between creating a Post-Nuptial Agreement, and having a divorce. We also talked about using their couples counseling as a forum for discussing finances, to broach the subject safely before discussing the details of their finances. And we talked about creating an estate plan, as a way for her both to gain a better picture of their current finances, and to simultaneously create Wills. That day, when she stood up to leave my office, she told me that now that she was equipped with the information she needed, she felt empowered to return home and have a very overdue conversation with her husband.

Determining the right path forward

Molly was at a juncture in her life that required her to carefully contrast the differences between her marriage's contribution to her current state of unhappiness and what impact a divorce would have on her life during the next many years.

Of utmost concern to me was John's history of verbal and physical abuse, and his heavy drinking. Molly assured me that except in the one instance she'd described to me, John had never physically abused her. In fact, she told me that he usually drank himself to sleep, and was more slovenly and uninspired than anything else. She told me that she did not live in fear of him and that she did not want to pursue a restraining order, even if they were to divorce. Her sentences were marked by alternating descriptions of anger at, and pity for John. Despite my usual skepticism about Molly's statements that John had never lifted a hand to her other than that one time she had described, I also considered that because she'd been in couples therapy with him for the past fifteen years, I could trust the therapist's assessment of whether there was any ongoing physical violence. I certainly wanted the therapist's assurance that, by living with John, Molly was not in any ongoing physical danger. If we could ascertain that she would be safe, I would then be comfortable working with her to assure that reinforcements were in place, both in terms of her therapist's awareness, and the creation of a safety plan for her in the event John did become violent.

Divorce or no divorce, John's illness demanded that Molly become informed about their finances. As women outlive men by a wide margin, more often than not at some point in their lives they become primarily responsible for the management of their own finances. Molly would not be the first woman to have that role thrust upon her without any preparation. However, knowing what she now knew, she understood the importance of creating an estate plan and how important it would be for her to have a working understanding of their finances; the lawyer creating the plan would be the one insisting on the disclosure, not Molly. Perhaps instead of seeing Molly as invading his sense of privacy, John could be led to understand the importance of creating a plan that minimized any future tax impact. In so doing, Molly could be given her own accounts to manage. If John resisted creating an estate plan, with the help of their couples therapist, Molly could then broach the subject of her need for some financial independence and the creation of her own account. If that option didn't work, we could help Molly to create a financial picture for herself: to understand their assets and debt, income and expenses. She could also set up a bank account in her own name, begin to deposit small sums of money into it, and thereby begin to get a sense of control over her finances. Instead of always relying on John for her "allowance," she would be freed up psychologically (even if initially the sums would be small).

At this juncture, a discussion of a Post -Nuptial Agreement (dividing assets between spouses while they remained married) seemed drastic, but Molly could keep it in mind as a measure to be taken if future dynamics between them made it necessary. Considering John's illness, it was also imperative that they create Powers of Attorney and Health Care Proxies so that in the event of his becoming incapacitated, she could help him carry out his wishes, and maintain their home and finances.

Final decisions--for now

Although I certainly didn't want Molly to feel trapped in her relationship with John, considering his health and life expectancy, what was likely to be a somewhat precarious state of their finances, and her lack of financial experience, to recommend they enter into what could become contentious and protracted negotiations didn't seem to me to be the best course of action. That being said, if Molly's safety were ever in danger, I would not want her to remain living in the same house with John. In fact, if John's health improved, and Molly gained some financial experience and independence during the course of the next year or so, and remained increasingly unhappy living with John, she could decide to pursue a divorce.

However, at this point in their lives, many other steps could be made to improve their situation. Divorce could actually worsen things for them. Additionally, if John's health worsened and he died while Molly was still married to him, she would stand to inherit a portion or perhaps all of his estate, whereas if they divorced, she would have lost much of the wealth they jointly acquired.

Like Molly, you need to define your goals and imagine the goals of your spouse. As an example, I will list Molly's expressed goals and those she imagined were John's. You can create your own goals in the workbook section of this book.

Molly's goals

- Create a safety plan for herself in the event John becomes abusive toward her;
- Gain clarity about her finances- to know what assets and debt she and her husband share, and what their income and expenses are on a monthly basis;
- Build a long term financial plan by working with a financial consultant;
- Open her own bank account and begin to fund it;
- Become informed about John's healthcare;
- Support John through his illness;
- Work with John to establish an Estate Plan;
- Become fully aware of her legal rights and responsibilities in the event that she wants to move forward toward a divorce in the future;
- Continue in couples counseling with John;
- Continue in individual therapy for her own support;

- Have enough independent money in the bank so that she is able to travel at will to see her children.

Molly's imagined goals of John:
- Maintain control over Molly and her life;
- Maintain control over their finances, and to not willingly inform Molly of same;
- Fight his cancer (Is his unwillingness to let Molly attend medical appointments a function of his fear that she'll see him as weak?);
- Build an Estate Plan if he could feel that it would give him control over himself and his property in the event he were to become incapacitated;
- Build an Estate Plan if he could be helped to articulate a legacy for his children;
- Continue in couples' counseling with Molly.

Will "litigation-lite" work for you?
When considering "litigation-lite," you must realize that it's still litigation, the traditional court involved process. Ask yourself:

- Do I feel like I do or might need Orders from the Court? (e.g., spousal or child support)
- Do I need more immediate definition around particular issues that I don't think my spouse is likely to agree to? (e.g., spousal or child support)
- Do I feel like I do or might need protection from the Court? (a restraining order for domestic violence)
- Do I feel like I might need a Court Order to curb financial spending or freeze a bank account?
- Do I feel as if my spouse might not voluntarily fully disclose information about finances that I currently don't know or have access to?
- Do I feel able or unable to speak directly to my spouse?

- Do I feel intimidated by my spouse?
- Does my spouse feel intimidated by me?
- Am I fearful of my spouse?
- Is my spouse fearful of me?
- Will I be likely to use this process to prolong our interactions?
- Will my spouse be likely to use this process as a means of prolonging our interactions?
- Will my spouse and I be able to create a Co-Parenting schedule or will we need the Court's assistance?

Your turn

Like Natasha and Molly, you need to define your goals and imagine those of your spouse. You also need to define what the Court can and cannot provide for you and your family. In order to help you do that, please turn to the workbook section of this book, **Part V (d)**.

PART IV

LITIGATION

James and Bobby

Initial contact

It had been less than a year since gay marriage had been legalized in Massachusetts when a gay man called my office seeking advice. In our first meeting, James told me that he and Bobby had been together for 17 years, and that they had intertwined their lives financially and in every single lifestyle decision they'd made.

…..or so he'd thought. Recently he'd learned that Bobby, the man he'd trusted and devoted himself to, the man he'd married among the first gay marriages to take place in Massachusetts, had betrayed him on a grand scale. Bobby had been living a second secret life that involved drugs, prostitutes, and the depletion of a great deal of their jointly acquired wealth.

James is an accomplished interior designer, and with his skill and business acumen he had renovated four homes, sold them for significant profits, and in turn invested those earnings into more stately homes. However, Bobby was a business consultant and the higher earner of the two. His income largely supported them and had allowed them to put away substantial savings toward their retirement. Although Bobby had always handled their investments, James had opened an investment company account, and noticed a number of irregularities on the statement; when he called their investment broker, he learned that Bobby had been withdrawing large sums on a regular basis.

Bobby had never mentioned any of these withdrawals to James. James confronted Bobby, who said he would move out. James hadn't asked him to move out, and he wasn't even sure he wanted him to. He only wanted to understand what was going on, how long Bobby had been lying to him, what he'd spent the money on, and if he'd contracted any sexually transmitted diseases. Bobby had fallen silent. He moved out the next day. He would not return phone calls or answer email. James had no idea where Bobby was until a mutual friend told him that he'd moved to New York City.

Background

For about 15 years before same-sex marriage was allowed in Massachusetts, James and Bobby had been living as a committed couple. James naturally believed that they were on solid footing. During the time they'd been together, they'd bought and sold multiple homes, always upgrading after James completed a top-to-bottom renovation. When I met James they owned two magnificent properties, a stately home on Beacon Hill in Boston and a summer house in Provincetown. James was in disbelief regarding what he'd discovered about Bobby's second life. He knew, however, that Bobby was spinning out of control. Bobby rejected James' offers to help, and told James he didn't want him involved in his life any longer.

First steps

James relayed to me that he thought Bobby was on a course of self-destruction. Despite his Ivy League education, advanced degrees in both science and math, and successful career, Bobby had been unsuccessful at accepting himself. In the seventeen years they'd been together, he'd never brought James home to meet his family; he'd never told his family he was gay or that he was living with James, and he existed in fear of their somehow finding out. James told me that he thought Bobby had been depressed for years and was now sublimating his depression and acting out in impulsive and harmful ways. The longer we talked, the more James was able to move beyond his empathy for Bobby and express his own feelings of hurt and betrayal. Within a couple of months of our having begun to work together, James began to see Bobby's having moved out as his last gift to him. James's focus was then able to turn to self-preservation, moving forward and getting divorced.

James needed to act quickly to keep Bobby from depleting money from their investment accounts. He needed Court orders and he needed them quickly. We needed to get him appropriate legal counsel and deal with the rest of the inevitable fallout. James was reeling from Bobby's deception and dishonesty, and he felt paralyzed about moving on with his own life. He would need to learn how to once again trust himself and his own judgment.

James's journey would be one of self-exploration and reflection. He was up to the task, but first we had to distill what were legal issues and what were psychological issues so that he wasn't seeking revenge and compensation from the wrong venues. Once that was accomplished, James was able to hire legal counsel to resolve the financial and legal issues, and begin therapy to try to understand more about how he'd arrived where he was, and how he wanted to move forward.

Next choices

As Bobby at first would not communicate with James, there was not any way to achieve a negotiated agreement between them. Bobby was furiously hemorrhaging money, so it was imperative to obtain a Court Order to try to put a tourniquet on his spending. Their jointly held investment account needed to be frozen. As James feared that Bobby's reckless behavior could result in lawsuits being filed against him, he also wanted to obtain sole title to the real estate they had acquired together. Furthermore, as he carried and was paying for Bobby's health insurance, he wanted permission to remove him from the policy or at least have the responsibility for its payment shift to Bobby. He also wanted to remove him as the beneficiary of his life insurance policy.

Finances were soon settled. Bobby didn't respond to any temporary Court Orders, so by default James was awarded both of their homes and the entire remaining assets in their investment account. He was then able to focus on himself and the reestablishment of his career. Instead of feeling victimized and vengeful, he felt empowered.

After Bobby received the final Court Order, he called James to see if they could reconcile. In James's mind, whether Bobby meant what he said or not didn't matter. What did matter is that he was clear in his own mind that he'd moved on and that the conversation Bobby was now suggesting was simply too little too late.

Results

Through it all, James remained composed and resolute. Although at first he *felt* vengeful, therapy helped him move beyond that and become intent on keeping his own life from spontaneous combustion. He didn't want an ugly fight, but he did want to maintain what he'd worked hard to achieve.

Our work together began with identifying James's aspirations, goals, and objectives. He needed to re-establish his own healthy self-identity, and envision a path toward wellness and growth. Some of this work was psychological, some financial, and some legal.

As Bobby would not communicate directly with James, filing a Complaint in Court through the traditional divorce process was the only appropriate mechanism to salvage the financial holdings they'd worked to achieve together, and to sever their ties so that they could both move on with their lives and into other potential relationships.

Therapy helped James withstand the trying nature of the divorce process. He didn't want to become "the poster child for gay divorce," so he carefully interviewed a number of lawyers. He didn't want to hire a high profile or gay lawyer, either of whom he feared could use his circumstances to gain publicity or raise their professional profile. He needed someone who would see his case in a very factual manner, and approach its resolution without fanfare and through the procedural mechanisms that exist to accomplish James's end goals. As Bobby refused to hire a lawyer and engage in any process of negotiating, the case had to be tried in Court. James hired a woman who was experienced and capable, but not flamboyant or inflammatory in her style or approach. Together we worked out a clear roadmap. Assets were frozen and a trial was held. Bobby never showed up for the trial and James was the only witness. James's lawyer skillfully put in the evidence, and all of their joint assets were transferred to James. In addition to both parcels of real estate and the entire investment account becoming James's property, he was allowed to stop making health insurance coverage payments on Bobby's behalf and remove him as a beneficiary of his life insurance policy.

James was ready to mourn the relationship and move on with his life.

James's goals

To create a safety plan for himself in the event Bobby returned angry and looking for retribution;

- To gain clarity about his finances, secure their assets (both real estate and financial portfolio) and keep Bobby from furthering their continued depletion;
- To assure his long term financial security by working with a financial consultant;
- To determine that he was physically healthy by getting tested for STD's;
- To limit his financial exposure to Bobby's reckless acts;
- To make sure that Bobby is responsible for his own health insurance;
- To continue/begin individual therapy, to gain perspective on the complications and ending of his marriage.

James' imagined goals of Bobby:

- To escape whatever marital responsibilities and obligations he owes to James;
- To be able to have continued access to their financial assets so that he can continue to drink, buy drugs, spend and live recklessly and to great abandon;
- To ignore any mutual financial obligations (e.g.- payment of mortgages and health insurance).

Choosing the right legal process

Because Bobby was being entirely uncommunicative with James, neither mediation, Collaborative Law nor arbitration were viable paths for them. In that sense, his decision was a simple one. The traditional court process was the only way he would be able to secure his rights, and his future.

For James, the key issue was hiring the right lawyer to most expeditiously accomplish the goals he had identified. Because Bobby was rapidly depleting their assets, and because obtaining Court orders quickly was necessary, I wanted James to immediately begin interviewing attorneys. We arranged three interviews for him over the course of the next three days; all of the attorneys had previously agreed that they could make an immediate Court appearance the following week, once James made a hiring decision.

James hired a seasoned, yet low-key attorney, and asked us to remain involved to ensure that his case proceeded in the manner and within the time frame we'd discussed.

The following week the attorney was in Court and obtained orders to freeze all Bobby's spending on their shared financial accounts. Even though notice of that action was sent to Bobby, he ignored it (as he did every further notification from the Court or from legal counsel). This case was unique in that it was a litigated case but one where Bobby chose not to appear or be represented. As a result, James' attorney was able to put on an unrebutted case; as only James' side was presented, the Judge made orders precisely in accordance with his demands.

Is the Litigation process right for you?

When considering this method, ask yourself:

- Do I feel as if I have *a full and fair understanding of our finances*?
- Do I have immediate and necessary *access* to our assets?
- Do I expect to be *sharing children and finances* in an on-going relationship with my soon-to-be former spouse?
- Will I be *restructuring* our family, or *severing ties*?
- Is *negotiation* with my spouse possible or is he or she disengaged from the process?

- Do I feel intimidated by my spouse, and do I need *protection from the Court* (financial or physical)?
- Am I fearful of my spouse and do I need the *"container"* of the Courtroom for protection?
- Do I trust my spouse to be honest and forthcoming with me, or do I think Court orders and other formal discovery procedures will be necessary to get to the *truth about our finances*?
- Will my spouse be compliant with agreements we make out of Court, or will Court orders be necessary to gain his or her compliance with obligations (e.g. child support and spousal support)?
- Will the Court process be likely to expedite outcomes, or be used by either me or my spouse as a process to *prolong interactions* between us?
- There are some situations that demand litigation and Court involvement. Safety of spouses and children is a paramount concern, and if you have any fear for your safety or that of your children, you should seek *immediate protection* through the Court.
- The following situations will require Court involvement:
  - Restraining orders;
  - An inability without Court Orders to gain a full and fair understanding of the parties' finances;
  - Feelings of intimidation;
  - A grounded belief that agreements between the parties will not be honored unless they are enforceable through Court Orders;
  - Your reluctance or fear of being in the same room with your spouse for prolonged discussions, or in the event a restraining order between the parties is currently in place;
  - Mental illness, alcohol or drug addiction(s) in one or both of you.

MEDIATION

Janet and Tom

Janet filed for divorce after eleven years of marriage to Tom. Janet and Tom met when they were in college, and married soon after. They have two children, ages five and eight. They have a relatively comfortable life – a house that they bought five years ago with mortgage payments that they can manage with both of their incomes, and two older cars that are paid off. Janet makes $50,000 per year as a nurse working thirty-two hours per week; Tom makes $60,000 per year as a firefighter.

When Janet filed for divorce, she did it without an attorney, hoping that she and Tom would be able to work things out. They had talked about it for almost a year before she filed, and they both seemed to acknowledge that they didn't hate each other, but that it just wasn't working out between them anymore. But since she filed, and he moved out, things have gotten more tense. Tom wants to see the children every day after school until he starts his 6:00 p.m. shift at work, and every Saturday. Tom works four days on/three days off. Janet is fine with Tom having a lot of time with the kids, but the schedule that he wants is really disruptive to meals, bedtime, and homework. Janet doesn't know how to approach Tom about doing something different for the kids. And her child care options have changed since Tom moved out. It used to be that each of the grandmothers would help with the kids, especially when Tom and Janet both had overnight shifts, which happens at least one to two times per month. Now, Tom's mom refuses to care for the kids when they are at Janet's house, and Janet's mom won't care for the kids at Tom's house. Janet's work schedule is most Saturdays overnight and 6:00 a.m. to 2:00 p.m. on three days per week.

Janet has noticed that the kids are struggling a bit, trying to figure out the new schedule and trying to be really, really good for each of their parents, but they seem stressed and distracted. For example, they keep leaving things at the wrong house, which is requiring trips across town on the way to and from school. And Janet and Tom have both found that their expenses have gone way up with the separation – he has an apartment and has reduced what he is paying toward the mortgage, and everyone is eating out more because things are so hectic in the evenings.

Janet wants to try to finish up the divorce on her own, without an attorney, but Tom keeps talking about getting an attorney to make sure he is not being "taken to the cleaners" and that his rights as a father are secure.

Both parents really care about their children, and about making sure that they each have a continuing relationship with the children. They know that it will be challenging to deal with their crazy work schedules, but they really just can't come up with a solution that works for them. Janet's goals are to maintain as positive a relationship as possible with Tom around parenting, and to have the children feel secure. Janet also wants to be sure that she is able to continue with her job, but knows that her schedule – and Tom's – can make that challenging for both of them and for the kids. It has worked because they have had the support of each of their mothers, but with the divorce, Janet is afraid that that mutual support could go away. Right now, though, Janet is not sure that they can talk to each other without it breaking down into tears and unhelpful arguments about what is "mine" and what is "yours," and what is best for the children. Janet would love to bring each of their mothers into a discussion about what they are able and willing to do in regard to caring for their grandchildren after the separation and divorce. What the grandmothers are able and willing to do will have a huge impact on what Janet's and Tom's respective work and parenting time schedules can be both in the short term and in the long run.

Janet thinks that Tom's goals are to make sure that he has time and a relationship with the children, though she knows that he is feeling a lot of pressure from his work and from his family. He is concerned about paying a lot in child support, and child care costs, which is something that they have not had to worry about until now, when they are faced with divorce and separation. Janet thinks that Tom's goals regarding maintaining family and child relationships, and not having the children feeling insecure are the same as hers, so she is hopeful that they will be able to talk things through.

Janet heard about mediation as a process and is interested in it but is not sure if it is right for Tom and her. Because they have such complicated work schedules, mediation could be a better process than litigation because they could sit down with the mediator and really think about what the possible schedules could be that could work for them. Janet is open to brainstorming all different options to try to make things work consistent with their goals, and hopes that Tom would be on board with that kind of open-minded approach if he really understood what was involved. Janet thinks it might be useful to bring each of the grandmothers into mediation at some point if there is a mediator willing to do that so that they can have all the options on the table and know what is possible around child care and arranging not just work schedules, but also figuring out time that the grandmothers could spend with the children.

Janet's goals
- Maintain as positive a relationship as possible with Tom around parenting;
- Have their children feel secure;
- Be sure that she is able to continue with her job;
- Maintain relationships with and support from their extended families.

Janet's imagined goals of Tom

- Make sure that he has time and a relationship with their children;
- Have their children feel secure;
- Have a manageable payment of child support, and predictable child care costs;
- Maintain relationships with and support from their extended families.

Because Janet and Tom's goals are similar in scope and they both are able to work well together, and in their children's best interest, mediation is a forum that will let them flush out the particular details of their children's needs without unnecessarily escalating issues in a more contentious framework. Then further, as Courts and Judges have limited time to address the detailed needs of families mediation is a more relaxed way in which to do this. Additionally, Janet and Tom's desire to involve their mothers in the scheduling of their children, is something that the Court would not be able to accommodate, but a mediator would likely work with them.

To determine if mediation might be right for you, turn to the end of this book where you will find your personal workbook and a quiz to help you assess the most likely best legal processes for you.

COLLABORATIVE LAW

Michael and Chanel

"This isn't the deal I thought I'd made. And it's not about us. It's about you and me."

Considering divorce

I first met with Michael and Chanel about a year after they had retreated from a contentious litigation process they had been embroiled in for more than six months. Having two young children and a lot of hope that they would be able to reconcile their differences, they had decided to stop the divorce process and redouble their efforts toward rebuilding their marriage and united family. Only a few months later, they hit another impasse, and that's when they ended up in my office. The one thing they could agree upon at that point was that they wanted to avoid an adversarial process.

At our initial meeting, Michael and Chanel told me that they presented a united front to the world. In fact, they said, they were "always together." However, just under the surface of that front were control issues and strife. Also, despite the rosy exterior they showed the world, they differed widely on values and aspirations for their children.

Many times, at this point in a couple's decision making, blame enters in. Chanel said that if only Michael were "nice to her," she would stay. She often felt "bullied" by Michael, overwhelmed by his ability to express himself, and angry at him for "talking over" her and failing to listen to her point of view. Michael repeatedly said that Chanel's spending was the reason he wanted to end the marriage, as he didn't know "another way to stop the bleeding." He didn't see how two people who wanted such different things out of life could make a marriage work. Michael had simple tastes, and spent much of his non-parenting time involved in charitable work. Chanel enjoyed a more upscale lifestyle: traveling and introducing her children to the "finer things in life."

Over time, the deeper we went, the more I learned about the reality of their finances. The situation wasn't as rosy as Chanel wished to believe. In fact, the money Michael had saved before their marriage was mostly spent; it was not a "bottomless pit" and Michael was quite aware of that. On the other hand, Chanel thought Michael should work harder and earn more, leaving the parenting to her, which in turn offended Michael. Soon, Chanel found a job and was earning as much as Michael, but that didn't resolve the money issue.

Still, for many months, neither Michael nor Chanel wanted to commit to proceeding toward divorce. Despite their differences, they were deeply enmeshed with one another, and had mutual respect on many levels. Chanel readily admitted that Michael was a good parent, and Michael felt the same way about Chanel. Michael refused to leave the house because he was concerned about access to the children, and Chanel was not willing to leave the house at all, and expected the children to remain with her. Nevertheless, they both wanted the children to maintain ongoing, positive relationships with both parents, and they hoped to restructure the family so that all of them would be better able to grow and thrive. They were both saddened that the marriage seemed unworkable.

Fortunately, both Michael and Chanel became willing to acknowledge and accept their differences and the contributions they had both made to the disintegration of their marriage. They harbored no ill will toward each other, and although they still had anger, they were able to set their emotions aside for the benefit of their children and the longer-term greater good of settling their differences.

Divorce or no divorce?

First of all, whether they were going to pursue the divorce or reconcile, Michael and Chanel needed a more realistic understanding of their
finances: Michael was afraid of ending up totally broke, and Chanel had
to recognize the limits of their assets. Together, we worked out how much
money they spent to support their current lifestyle, and discussed possible
future asset and support provisions should they divorce. Only then could
Michael begin to grapple with the possibility of his moving out and finding
a suitable second home for him and their children. Life after divorce now
seemed imaginable.

That accomplished, we then discussed their concerns about telling the children. They had enormous trepidation about it. They wanted to consider
their ages, developmental differences, likely reactions, and support systems
(friends, other family members, teachers, coaches, and potential therapists). We worked together to develop language they felt was mutual, and
to anticipate what questions and reactions the children might have **(see V
(b) for example script)**. They decided to talk to the children during their
winter break from school, after Christmas, which they had agreed to spend
together. That way, the children would have some time to process the news
and adjust to the idea of change before going back to school.

Throughout these discussions, both wanted to be heard equally; separate
meetings with Michael and Chanel allowed them to be honest about what
was most important to them in the short and long term. Working with
checklists and contributing individual input, they independently rated
both priorities and goals should they stay with their decision to divorce:

Michael

- Amicably resolve the divorce;
- "Get a grip" on the finances, short and long term;
- Maintain a deep and satisfying relationship with the children;

- Facilitate as much as possible their children's growth into secure, independent adults;
- Develop a good working co-parenting relationship with Chanel;
- Protect his finances from Chanel's "frivolous" spending.

Chanel

- Amicably resolve the divorce;
- Maintain a deep and satisfying relationship with the children;
- Develop a good working co-parenting relationship with Michael;
- Facilitate the children's growth into secure and independent adults;
- Grow her career;
- Develop a new relationship with a partner, in which she no longer felt smothered and unheard.

With these needs, goals, and priorities in mind, they were ready to be guided toward appropriate forms of dispute resolution and to take concrete steps toward amicably restructuring their family.

Choosing the right legal process

Even before they had met me, Michael and Chanel had determined that litigation was not for them. However, because Chanel often felt "bullied" by Michael, and was fearful that he would try to cut her out of monies to which she was entitled, mediation without lawyers present was also not the right way to move forward. They weren't familiar with the Collaborative Law option, but were open to learning about it.

I explained to them that the Collaborative model involves five people— the parties themselves, each of their lawyers, and a coach. The coach is a therapist trained to act as a neutral professional who can facilitate the negotiation process. Unlike the lawyer, whose job is to represent her client's position and help the parties resolve their problems, the coach is able to observe issues and smooth impasses as they arise between the parties and the lawyers. The coach is trained to be a facilitator, and to recognize when anyone—client or lawyer—becomes positional or oppositional, and to then reorient the process so that it can remain focused on resolution.

Although many lawyers are able to negotiate settlements successfully on behalf of their clients, the Collaborative process differs in significant ways. First, the clients are present at and involved in every meeting, and they are expected to be participants, as opposed to recipients of information from their lawyers who advocate for them, and then later provide them with the information. Instead, lawyers support them as active participants, and ensure their legal interests are understood and well expressed.

Lawyers who engage in the Collaborative Law process also sign an Agreement with one another that stipulates they will go to court only with the clients once there is an agreement ready for the court to approve, or for other mutually agreed upon provisions and/or orders. As a result, going to court cannot be used as a means to resolve a dispute; parties must struggle through resolving their disagreements in order to continue on in this process. In addition, if the process is unsuccessful, the parties must hire other lawyers to represent them. We only recommend the Collaborative process if the parties have an excellent chance of resolving their differences in this model. We also set up check-in points at which we discuss with clients— and sometimes lawyers, if they agree—to assess how well the process is working, so the parties don't waste time and money.

Sometimes, eighty percent of a problem can be resolved through the Collaborative process, and reaching that point is a success, not a failure. It can shorten a process that could have been much more protracted, less productive, and more expensive.

Once Michael and Chanel understood the Collaborative process, they thought it would suit them both, and they decided to interview lawyers to hire. We arranged meetings for them with lawyers we thought would be well suited to them, both in terms of the skill needed and individual personalities. Chanel liked the first lawyer she interviewed and hired him. Michael was less sure. He didn't want to sign an agreement that would limit his ability to make interim financial decisions, especially anything that would prevent his buying another home.

It became increasingly apparent that Michael was still ambivalent about getting divorced. We recommended them to a highly skilled couples therapist, and they committed to doing some intensive work with her.

Final decisions

Working with a therapist doesn't always result in reconciliation, but can help the parties deal with the reality of irreconcilable differences. They returned to my office still equivocating about whether to get divorced. I gently asked them what they truly wanted.

"I'm so unhappy, and feel hopeless," Michael blurted out. "I don't think it will ever be better for me in this marriage." Chanel cried, and said she wished things were different but she was already beginning the process of mourning the end of their relationship.

That week, Michael put an offer in on a house and it was accepted. He immediately called me in a panic, wanting to give the marriage another try. Chanel agreed. However, it was not to be.

What had they discovered through their hard work? No matter how much they wished they didn't have to end the marriage, Michael was positive it would never work for him, and Chanel accepted that they hadn't rushed into the decision, but had taken every avenue toward certainty.

Michael again started a home search, and he again found one he liked. This time he went through with it. He would move in about a month after closing and making renovations.

Without entering litigation or becoming adversarial, they knew they had made this decision carefully and consciously.

Can the Collaborative process work for you?

When considering this method, ask yourself:

- Do I feel as if I have a full and fair understanding of our finances?
- If sharing children and finances do I anticipate having an on-going relationship with my soon-to-be former spouse?
- Am I invested in optimizing our restructured family?
- Do I want to be actively involved in the negotiation of the divorce agreement?
- Do I feel intimidated by my spouse and/or does my spouse feel intimidated by me?
- Am I fearful of my spouse and/or is my spouse fearful of me?
- Do I trust my spouse to be honest and forthcoming with me?
- Do I want to grapple with these issues in the presence of my spouse, and/or will my spouse want to grapple with them in my presence?
- Do I need more immediate definition around particular issues that I don't think my spouse is likely to agree to (e.g. spousal or child support)?
- Will I be tempted to use this process to prolong interaction with my spouse, and/or will my spouse be tempted to use the process to prolong interaction with me?

There are multiple situations in which the Collaborative process will not work, and all are pertinent and must be considered relative to both parties.

- Restraining orders
- Lack of understanding of finances
- Feelings of intimidation
- Lack of understanding of legal rights

- Distrust around finances or honoring mutual agreements
- Reluctance to be in the same room for prolonged discussions or in the event a restraining order between the parties is currently in place
- Alcohol or drug addiction(s) in one or both of you
- Unmedicated/unstable mental illness

The Collaborative process is not a guarantee of an easy road—in fact, it's very likely it will be bumpy, but then, which choice isn't? Having supports in place will go a long way toward providing perspective, comfort, and understanding.

Supports for children

Even though Michael and Chanel anticipated and discussed with me the difficult process of telling their children about Michael's move and the divorce, and we had considered a wide range of possible emotions, their eleven-year-old son Caleb's reaction surprised them. He became hostile, running outside, filling his hands with dirt, and returning screaming. He threw the dirt around the house and yelled, "You have ruined our family, and now I'm going to ruin our house." Eventually, he needed to be physically restrained.

Because we had preemptively spoken to a therapist for their son, he was able to be seen quickly, and had a safe place to express his anger, sadness, and disappointment. However, as time went on, he became less willing to see the therapist. He also refused to spend time with his dad, and told his father he wouldn't even talk to him again until he moved back into the house.

Because Michael and Chanel had identified upfront their shared goal of having a deep and satisfying relationship with both of their children and good Co-Parent relationships with one another, they were able to talk through the situation with Caleb and work together with professionals about how best to help him work through his grief.

Chanel initially felt secretly pleased that Caleb had "sided" with her. However, she was able to see that as a long-term plan, Caleb's behavior wouldn't serve him well, nor would it truly be a good plan for her. At one point, we had a conversation about the differences between having a very attached eleven-year-old and a very attached thirty-year-old son, one perhaps unable to form an intimate relationship with another adult due to an overly enmeshed relationship with his mother. Chanel could quickly see that in the long run having Caleb on "her side" now would not be useful to him or to her.

Meanwhile, Michael was devastated and wracked with guilt about what his decision had done to Caleb. He also had feelings of sadness and anger, yet he knew he couldn't let the emotions of his eleven-year-old son dictate the adult decisions he'd thought so long and hard about.

Michael didn't let Caleb's preferences deter him from attending Caleb's basketball games. He persisted in asking Caleb to go with him to the library to do homework, or out for pizza, and restrained himself (with great difficulty) from expressing his frustration if Caleb rejected his offers. Month after month, Michael hung in there, imagining himself the oak tree Caleb would need for support. He never let Caleb's behavior undermine his ability to show him unconditional love.

Eventually, somehow, one day Caleb agreed to go to the library with his dad. They had what Michael described as an "alright" time, and the next week Caleb was the one to ask Michael to go out for pizza, including one of Caleb's friends. Michael was thrilled, and they had a fine time. After pizza, Michael asked Caleb if he and his friend wanted to come over to his house to shoot hoops in the driveway. Much to his surprise, the boys took him up on the offer.

The summer was now upon them. With school out, Michael and Chanel created a schedule that included overnights for Caleb and their daughter, Lily, at both homes.

Lily adapted much more easily than Caleb, but Michael and Chanel remained alert and vigilant to the fact that she might be keeping her emotions in check for the moment, only later to act out in ways that weren't predictable right now. That having been said, in nearly all cases with the right foresight and support, parents discover with admiration how resilient children can be.

Reweaving the tapestry

Because Michael and Chanel had articulated their commitment to resolve the divorce amicably, they worked together to help Caleb. They learned fast and furiously the importance of a good Co-Parenting relationship, and made the shift as quickly as they could.

Even though multiple patterns were disrupted, that summer, they were well on their way to a newly restructured family.

LAWYER ASSISTED NEGOTIATION
Collaboratively Minded Lawyers and Collaborative Law

Theresa and David

First contact

Unlike most clients when I first meet them, Theresa seemed invigorated, even happy. She told me that she'd recently met someone and had fallen in love. Her surprise was that after twenty years of having been married to a man, she'd fallen in love with a woman. For the first time in her life she felt comfortable in her own skin. She felt alive, authentic, and bursting with joy.

Theresa knew this euphoria wouldn't last, but she also recognized that it was time for change. She worried about how her children would react to her coming out and how angry her husband was likely to be. She wondered if being gay could somehow be used against her in the custody of her children and in the payment of spousal and child support.

Background

Theresa told me she'd been unhappily married for many years, and that her being gay wasn't the primary reason for her unhappiness, and only part of the reason for her wanting to be divorced. She said that her husband, David was controlling and difficult, unhelpful with their three children, and cold toward her.

Theresa had only practiced medicine for a year before she and David began having children and deciding--together with her husband--that she would give up her career, at least for awhile, to become a stay-at-home mom. David was also a doctor, and whereas they lived primarily off his income, they also occasionally dipped into the interest earned (and sometimes principal) from a Trust Fund his parents had created for them. The children attended private school and had trust funds for their college educations. Although Theresa was very close with her children, then ages 11, 15, and 17, she worried that they might be disconcerted or even alienated by learning she was gay. I asked whether she thought any of the children were gay, and she told me that she thought one could be. In actuality, Theresa's decision to come out might ease her son's own development and comfort with his sexual identity.

Additional complications existed through a Prenuptial Agreement and Trust Theresa had signed the day before her and David's wedding. That timing raised concerns for me, and when I asked her more about it, she explained that David's parents had arrived from Australia a week before their wedding and insisted that they sign a Prenuptial Agreement prior to being married--basically, "sign this, or no wedding." At the time Theresa had been only 25 years old and wanted very much to marry David.

Theresa scrambled to find a lawyer to review the Agreement and ultimately hired someone who worked with her sister. Although the lawyer reviewed the Agreement, no negotiations took place between Theresa and David's family's lawyer. She stated that the balance of power had not been even. David's family had obviously been concerned about protecting their enormous wealth, although they told Theresa it was for her protection as well. Reading through the Agreement, I found it apparent that Theresa had given up far more than she had received. Whether a Court would find the Agreement to be valid was an important question in terms of both marital asset division and ongoing support for Theresa. Support would be very important as she wasn't interested in resuming her medical career; she described having lost both skills and interest in practicing. Instead, she was interested in pursuing a career in the visual arts. Having taken art courses over the years, she had developed real skill, and she was working with a gallery on a show of her work.

Theresa wondered what role her sexuality would play in the settlement. She wondered if perhaps she shouldn't even mention it and just get divorced for all the rest of her reasons. However, she wanted to live authentically.

First Steps

Once Theresa understood the Court would not penalize her based on her sexual orientation, she gave herself permission to talk to her children and her husband about her sexuality and to then proceed with the divorce.

The children had many questions for her. David didn't see her sexual orientation as a problem, and instead thought they should continue to live as roommates, and simply have other romantic relationships. That was untenable for Theresa as her sexual orientation wasn't the only or even primary source of her marital unhappiness, and moving out and on was unequivocal in her mind.

Creating a Co-Parenting arrangement was also of utmost importance to her. Theresa was relieved to learn that parties' sexuality is not a factor in child custody in Massachusetts, where gay marriage is legal. If she and David were unable to resolve their differences and the Court were asked to decide on the custody arrangement, her having been a stay-at-home mom, the primary caretaker of the children, and involved in their education, social, and emotional development would be the pertinent factors a Court would consider.

Although Theresa was involved with a woman, she said she would never consider uprooting her children and moving, or living with someone else while her children were still at home. Clearly, her sexual identity was not the primary reason to end the marriage at that moment in time. Therefore, portraying it as the primary reason for the divorce wasn't a good option: it would seem artificial, inflammatory, unnecessary, and probably disruptive in terms of reaching a settlement. Prior to delving into an issue that would take time for the family to adjust to and accommodate, it was more important to prioritize custody and to resolve the other legal and financial issues.

First and foremost, it was important to find legal counsel that was equipped to understand the financial complications of the Trust and the Prenuptial Agreement and how those factors would play out in terms of a marital asset division and ongoing spousal and child support. Theresa stood to acquire a substantial distribution from the Trust, so whether and how much to contest the validity of the Prenuptial Agreement would need to be weighed in contrast to any potential distribution from the Trust. Pragmatics and expenses of contesting the Prenuptial Agreement were important factors.

Moving forward legally

The questions we had to address were:

- Would David be interested in being a part of ongoing negotiations?
- Would he want to participate in mediation?
- Would he be interested in the Collaborative Law model?

Theresa was adamant that David would want nothing to do with the process, but as our process unfolded it turned out that she was incorrect about that. Despite his initial anger, something Theresa predicted, he recognized the futility in fighting about their jointly acquired property. Although she'd predicted he would insist on the traditional litigation framework and behave grudgingly, with a goal of paying as little as possible and moving on from there, instead he wanted to be actively involved in the settlement negotiations.

Sometimes, the facts of a case may seem more complicated than the actual resolution. Collaboratively-minded lawyers (which is not to be confused with Collaborative Law Practice Lawyers) who also have the capacity and interest in litigating if necessary are often, as in this case, the right choice. Fortunately, Theresa and David together were able to hire legal counsel who could effectively and expeditiously resolve their differences.

Other considerations

Theresa's case was for many reasons more complicated than the norm. Whereas therapy is almost uniformly recommended for anyone undergoing the challenges of a divorce, as well as for their children, Theresa's coming out as gay to her family added another layer of complexity. It was important for Theresa, David and their children to begin therapy as soon as possible so that they could have an immediate forum to discuss their family's upcoming changes and new dynamics.

PART V: LEGAL PATHS

As I actualize, I uncover. –Martin Buber

A. The Collaborative Process

Unlike conventional divorce, which relies upon the Court system as the backbone of the divorce process, the Collaborative Process is private and driven by the agendas of the clients and their lawyers. Although in both contexts your lawyer will try to obtain the best possible settlement for you, a lawyer who has agreed to represent you in the Collaborative Process is likely to see herself first and foremost as a "problem solver", rather than as an "advocate". Please note that Collaborative Law is not allowable in all states. To see if Collaborative Law is an option for you, call your state's Bar Association.

Collaborative lawyers are committed to helping you reach an out-of-court settlement. In fact, they agree *not* to represent you if the case does proceed to an adversarial court action. By contrast, in a conventional divorce the attorney generally starts with the adversarial process through a court filing, or with a position letter which, if not accepted, then leads to a court filing. Either way, the traditional divorce process starts with court and then moves to settlement and negotiation. The Collaborative Process starts with negotiation and settlement, before proceeding to court.

The Collaborative model mindset shifts lawyers' thinking from "if your only tool is a hammer, everything looks like a nail," to one that is solution-oriented. By focusing on alternatives to traditional adversarial methods, lawyers are engaged to help clients expand their settlement options. Collaborative professionals believe they can do this best by maintaining control over the sequence of agreements, rather than by seeing a difficult impasse as time to ask a judge to make an important decision for individuals and their families.

The Team

In a Collaborative case, clients work with a team of collaboratively-trained professionals. Their goal is to reach an out-of-court settlement, which will be presented to the court for final approval. Each party will be assisted by an attorney, and together they will hire a coach/facilitator (who is a mental health professional) and if needed, a financial neutral, child specialist, or other professional experts. Each of these team members plays a vital role in the Collaborative Process. Unlike a judge, the Coach is not a decision-maker. Rather, her role is to facilitate the Collaborative Process for the clients and their lawyers. Unlike a conventional divorce process, clients will always be present when their attorneys are negotiating.

In a conventional divorce, either client can file publicly accessible complaints, counter-claims, affidavits, motions, oppositions or memoranda arguing their allegations and positions. In the Collaborative Process, only a limited number of documents are filed with the court, and *only* when both clients agree.

Like many things in life, there are advantages and disadvantages to different approaches; Collaborative Law is no different. Some of its advantages include:

- Creating an atmosphere in which spouses can cooperate on terms of mutual respect;
- Removing the threat of litigation, allowing both parties and their collaborative attorneys to remain focused on solving problems;
- Coach intervention in the management of emotions that might otherwise derail, prolong, or prevent settlement;
- Joint retention of experts (*i.e.*, a financial specialist, or business appraiser) who will work for both parties, which saves costs, and avoids any "battle experts."

But this approach has its challenges as well.

- If each party has different views of the pace at which their case should proceed, it is unlikely that the spouses will agree about the speed at which their case is being handled;
- If one or both parties feel that going to court is inevitable, they are unlikely to see the process as a viable solution;
- If one of the parties is intimidated by the other, he or she will not be able to engage in the Collaborative Process;
- If there is a history of domestic violence, the Collaborative Process may not be a realistic option;
- If there is concern that one or both of the parties will not willingly and fully disclose their financial or other critical information.

The Collaborative Attorney

- Represents her client's interests, taking into account both parties' interests and those of the family as a whole;
- Refrains from using adversarial techniques;
- Educates the client about legal issues;
- Works effectively with the other spouse's attorney and coach/facilitator to create a new structure that maximizes settlement potential and aims to foster a healthy post-divorce environment.

The Collaborative Coach

- Serves as a neutral focused on managing process, behavior, and emotions;
- Provides expert advice on the psychology of divorce;
- Identifies and reinforces effective communication between parties;
- Intervenes to contain and manage conflict;
- Educates the attorneys about the parties' communication dynamics.

The Neutral Financial Professional

During the Collaborative process, the parties may choose to engage a neutral financial specialist, who can:

- Work for both parties, using agreed-upon financial documentation;
- Provide tax analysis so both parties will stay appraised of relevant financial details;
- Generate financial projections for post-divorce, so that the parties can evaluate how their lives (and budgets) will or will not need to change;
- Evaluate short- and long-term financial consequences of the decisions being made by the divorcing parties.

The Child Specialist

If parents are unable to agree on how to best serve the needs of their children, they may choose to jointly engage a child specialist, who can advise them, provide assistance specific to their child[ren]'s needs, and ease the child[ren]'s transition between environments.

Other Professionals

During the Collaborative Process, the parties may choose to engage other neutral professionals to assist with specific areas that require particular expertise (*e.g.*, valuations of real estate, businesses, or professional practices).

B. Litigation

In every divorce case, documents must be filed with a court to make the divorce final, and legally recognized by your state. When we talk about the process of litigation, we are focusing on cases that require more court involvement than the initial filing, and that of the final paperwork. If spouses cannot agree on important issues, they might opt to have a judge decide those details. Simply put: litigation is the default process for finalizing a divorce, but the fact that it is a default does not mean that it is a failure to have a case, or some issues in a case, go to litigation. The process of litigation is a way to resolve contested issues in a divorce case by allowing a judge to decide issues on your behalf.

Litigation is the most common process for divorce. In litigation, you literally "go to court" and have someone (a judge) decide things for you. The judge hears the evidence, applies the law, and issues orders regarding the things you disagree about.

You can have a judge decide all of the issues in your case (*e.g.*, alimony, property and debt division, parenting time/custody, decision-making, and child support) or only those issues that you have trouble agreeing on with your spouse. Litigation might follow mediation, or Collaborative settlement conferences that have been unable to settle the parties' differences.

Divorcing couples are sometimes able to solve disagreements regarding their children through mediation, but they continue to disagree about whether alimony should be paid, or for how long. In that case, the judge would be presented evidence only on the issues regarding alimony, and not on issues concerning the children. While you might think that if you can't resolve your case without taking the case in front of a judge that you have somehow failed, that is not at all true. Some issues can't be resolved without a hearing in front of a judge, and other issues should not be.

What is Litigation?

As noted in the overview, litigation is taking a case to court. Unlike in civil or criminal trials, there is no jury in a divorce case; the judge is the sole finder of fact. The parties, generally through attorneys, present their evidence to the judge, who will apply the law and decide the case. The advantage of litigation is that it can be used when there is no ability of the parties to resolve gnarly issues they will not ever be able to agree on. It provides an answer to the dispute, although it may not be an answer that either party would necessarily want. Litigation can be useful where one party is determined that he or she is correct and is unable or unwilling to compromise, or where compromise would be giving up too much or would otherwise not be appropriate, such as in cases involving domestic violence, child abuse, or neglect concerns. Litigation can also be useful when one or both parties really just need (or want) someone with authority to decide the issues upon which they disagree.

Taking a case before a judge to decide can be costly if attorneys are involved. The cost of taking a divorce case to a hearing can vary quite a bit, depending on many factors, amongst them are where you live, the issues that need to be addressed, and whether any expert witnesses are needed. While you can represent yourself in court at a hearing in a divorce case, you should keep in mind that you will be expected to know the rules of evidence and those of the court. If you don't follow those rules, the evidence you want to get before the judge could be excluded.

Evidence might include testimony from witnesses, expert testimony, and documents. Any of those types of evidence may include hearsay (*i.e.*, gossip – "He told me that…") that the judge will not consider. In most places, the statements that the children make will be considered hearsay and may not be testified to in court. If you decide to represent yourself in court, you should find local resources to help you. Many courts have electronic or in-person resources that can help you understand the process. In some states, you can hire an attorney for the limited purpose of helping you with paperwork or appearing in court for the hearing.

A judge has limited time to hear each case, so you should plan your time wisely. The judge will focus on what needs to be decided, so your presentation of the evidence should highlight those issues. In a court hearing, you will have to convey years of relationship-history in a matter of hours to the judge, and convey to him only the information that is important for him to decide the issues where you disagree.

The judge will look at the statutes and case law to decide what is relevant to your case; you should look at those statutes, too. In most states, there are "best interests factors" that the judge will use to guide her decision regarding parenting time and decision making. While those factors are often very general, they tend to have logical relevance to a child's life – e.g., how well the child is adjusted to his home, school, and community; how the parents are able to work together for the child's interests and set aside their own interests; how far apart the parents live from each other and how that practical limitation may affect parenting time. On the other hand, the judge does not need to know about the entire history of your relationship to decide issues of property division, or how hard your pregnancy was. In other words, you should be able to connect the evidence you want to present to a specific factor or element of the law in order for the judge to consider it.

The judge

The judge hears the evidence (facts), decides what evidence is applicable and credible, and applies the legal standards (e.g., best interests of the child, or the considerations for alimony) to those facts. Before a final hearing, you might have a Temporary Orders hearing or a series of case-management meetings to narrow down the relevant issues for the final hearing. Those meetings may be with the judge or with other court personnel.

The hearing

In addition to the judge, each spouse and their respective attorneys will be present. At the final hearing, witnesses may be subpoenaed (*i.e.,* ordered to come to court to testify), including expert witnesses who will charge a fee for their time.

What to think about before the final hearing

Judges find it helpful if the parties provide a written summary of their positions on each issue in dispute, copies of court orders (such as temporary child support or parenting time orders), or agreements that you have already made, any financial documents that you think would be helpful (such as any financial affidavits, or that you would be required to file with the Court and any other evidence that would help the judge best understand the financial resources and disputes).

C. Mediation

Mediation is a process that can be used before or after filing a complaint for divorce. In some Courts, judges will require you to participate in mediation before your case will be set for trial. Mediation is a private process where the spouses (generally with their attorneys present) will try to settle the issues regarding property division, debt division, alimony/maintenance, child support, parenting time, and decision making. Unlike a strict litigation process, there is more ability to make agreements in mediation that may not otherwise be able to be decided by the judge if the case goes to trial. For instance, some people will use mediation to discuss very particular issues regarding parenting (*e.g.,* the children's bedtime and who will take care of the children if they are sick and have to be out of school), or issues concerning maintenance that a court can't decide but the parties can (*e.g.*, specific and gradually stepping-down modifications to family lifestyle over the years that maintenance is in effect). It is important to note that if a divorcing couple decides to mediate without attorneys present, prior to embarking on the process they should each consult with a separate attorney for advice particular to their circumstances.

Those issues will not (or cannot) be addressed by the judge in a typical divorce case.

It is important to note that if a divorcing couple decides to mediate without attorneys present, prior to embarking on the process they should each consult with a separate attorney for advise particular to their circumstances.

What is Mediation?

Mediation is a confidential process by which the parties jointly hire a divorce mediator who serves as a "neutral." The mediator's role is to assist the parties in reaching an agreement, not to decide the issues for them or, generally speaking, to make recommendations as to what the mediator thinks you should do. Mediation is designed to be forward-reaching, rather than backward-looking; that is, looking at solutions to the issues, rather than assigning blame. In short, mediation is a process that can help in a divorce by bringing focused attention on alternative, appropriate, and self-directed solutions.

Process of Mediation

1. The Players

   Who is at the mediation:

   a. **The Mediator.**

   The mediator is generally an attorney or a mental health professional, but may not be either one – just someone who is trained and skilled in negotiation and problem solving through the mediation process. The mediator may be court-appointed, or selected by you and your spouse. In co-mediation, two mediators work together. Often in co-mediation, one of the mediators is an attorney and the other mediator is a therapist. Their dual perspectives can help to smooth the process of restructuring the family-future.

b. You and Your Spouse.

c. Attorneys. You may decide that you want to have your attorneys there, or you may decide not to. Generally, it is up to the parties whether attorneys will attend.

Support person/ domestic violence advocate. In some instances, particularly if there are issues of domestic violence in the relationship, you might have a support person (an advocate, for example) at the mediation with you. However, before bringing an advocate, you should check with the mediator to let them know that you are bringing someone and why. *If there is any issue related to domestic violence, raise that with the mediator well before the mediation. A good mediator should ask about those kind of safety concerns, and plan for them with you.*

Witnesses, experts, and children generally are not included in mediation, although if the particular situation warrants, it may be useful to have a financial advisor or accountant with each party. If you are not sure whether anyone other than the parties and the mediator will or should be present, contact the mediator before mediation to find out what they recommend. For example, you may meet with just the mediator and your spouse in an initial session and then in later sessions include other professionals such as financial advisors.

2. Before the Meeting

a. **What to bring to mediation** Some mediators will tell you what to bring to mediation. Generally, what mediators find helpful is a summary of your position on each issue that is in dispute, copies of court orders (such as temporary child support or parenting time orders) or prior agreements, any financial documents that you think would be helpful (such as financial affidavits required to file with the court. Even if you are using mediation before you file the divorce case in court, you should complete the financial affidavit to help you and the mediator understand what the financial resources and disputes are. Again, if you are not sure what you should bring, ask the mediator to help guide you.

b. **Identify any concerns about safety and let the mediator know ahead of time.** Most mediators are aware that there can be domestic violence issues between divorcing parties, and that those issues can make it hard for one person to fully participate in the mediation. Good mediators know that those issues can encompass physical violence, financial control, unstated intimidation. If you feel that you will not be able to fully participate in mediation and express yourself fully or honestly with the mediator, even in private (caucus) sessions with the mediator, then mediation may not be for you. If you want to try mediation or if you are ordered to participate in mediation, then talk to the mediator ahead of time about your concerns, and work with the mediator so that you clearly understand the mediator's obligation for confidentiality, and develop a safety plan for before, during, and after mediation. Mediation safety planning can include: having the mediation at a courthouse or other location with security; having a non-verbal signal for when you need a break; bringing with you an advocate or support person or therapy animal; having the mediator "own" your ideas or requests as his or her own suggestions for resolution; requesting to use "shuttle mediation" for all or part of the mediation process. Shuttle mediation is where the mediator moves between the parties who are in separate rooms.

c. **Establish realistic goals.** Before the mediation meeting, you should prepare by outlining what you want to accomplish in the mediation. It could be as specific as "I'd like to come away with an agreement on how to sell the house," or as general as "I'd like to be able to say what I want without feeling intimidated."

Going into a mediation, you might think that the mediation seems like it is scheduled for too long, but the process itself requires a commitment of time to present issues, sort out priorities and needs for each party, and to develop realistic solutions – as a mediator, I had many clients come into mediation concerned that two hours for the first session was much too long, only to have them be surprised at how quickly the time had passed when I said "Time's up."

3. During the Meeting

a. **Introduction to the process.** The mediator generally begins by outlining the process, and identifying the role that the mediator plays in the case. You may be asked to sign a mediation agreement that outlines the mediator's role and confidentiality obligations, and your financial obligations to the mediator. Keep in mind that although mediation is confidential, mediators generally have a duty to report threats to oneself or others or suspected child abuse or neglect, even if the information is shared with the mediator in the context of the mediation session. Often, the mediator will give each party an opportunity to tell his or her side of the story (and curtail rambling or blaming, so as to stay focused on the issues that need to be resolved). This helps the parties identify their points of dispute, and suggests an appropriate negotiation process. Unlike in an attorney assisted negotiation, the spouses will be the ones doing most of the talking during the mediation.

b. **Techniques.** During the mediation, the mediator may use a variety of techniques to help people feel comfortable talking about issues. The mediator may lay out "ground rules" before mediation, such as taking turns talking, asking the parties to verbally reflect back on what was said to show that they were listening and understanding each other; talking individually with each person in a meeting (called a "caucus"), summarizing the process and agreements as the session progresses; writing up agreements and having parties sign them or discuss them with their attorneys before signing the agreements; and suggesting next steps in the process.

c. **Agreements in mediation.** The mediator or the attorneys may write up agreements made during mediation for the parties to sign.

4. After the Meeting

a. Generally, it is up to the parties to file their final agreements with the court as part of the divorce process. The mediator, as a confidential neutral, does not file agreements or testify in court concerning these agreements.

    b. Mediation can be either ongoing or used for particular issues. Even after the divorce is finalized, mediation can be used to address issues that might come up later (i.e. parenting time or child support).

Mediation will be most effective when parties are willing to discuss the issues and honestly present information and positions. Mediation keeps you in control of the process and decisions being made; litigation leaves the final decisions to a judge.

Mediation may be more cost-effective than Collaborative Law and can be used on an as-needed basis as intractable issues come up before, during, and after the divorce case. However, it is important for the parties to recognize that the mediator is a neutral party and may not advise either party of their legal rights or responsibilities.

D. Arbitration

Unlike the public forum of a Courtroom, arbitration is a private setting, which is a significant reason some people prefer it. It's a venue for people to resolve disputes when they agree they disagree on the issues, and agree that someone other than themselves will be better able to bring clarity to their situation. In instances when a publicly aired dispute or the people involved in it might attract attention the parties would rather avoid, arbitration can be especially desirable.

Arbitrators are experienced practitioners, oftentimes retired judges. They can create a private courtroom setting where clients are able to set the time schedule with the arbitrator, and the parties and their lawyers can present the facts as they see them to be. Confidentiality provisions should be signed by everyone who testifies in an arbitration. The Arbitrator can streamline the process and make an Order that the parties agree will be binding. Only if the Arbitrator makes findings beyond the scope of the issues, is the Order appealable. It is important to recognize that Arbitration is unlike a Case Evaluation, which the parties can enter into for guidance and a non-binding decision.

The arbitration process can be used to more speedily overcome a stumbling block, for instance the division of multiple parcels of real estate, so that the parties can then move on to more amicably reach their remaining agreements.

Unlike Courts, arbitrators can untangle a dilemma within a mutually agreeable timeframe. Although unlike Courts this process is private pay, when finances allow it can be useful for the resolution of issues that otherwise left to fester could become a more complicated rift.

Another difference between the public litigation process and arbitration is that prior to engaging an arbitrator the parties can interview potential arbitrators and ask specific questions about the issue(s) they're looking to resolve; For instance, "What is your view of the law relative to the division of inherited money after separation of the parties?"

E. Case Evaluation

Case Evaluation is an opportunity for parties and their lawyers to ask a seasoned family law attorney or a retired family law judge for his or her opinion and guidance relative to disagreements or hurdles encountered while trying to reach an agreement. The opinion offered or decision recommended by the Case Evaluator is non-binding. In addition, where a case has issues related to children (parenting time or decision-making, for example), sometimes the Case Evaluation process can include not just an attorney or retired judge, but also mental health professionals who can help guide the parties' thinking in regard to the children

F. Attorney Negotiation

Negotiation between attorneys on your behalf is a process that emphasizes privacy and the importance of your position, but can often minimize communication and control because your views and positions are translated through other people. Depending on the complexity of the issues in a case, this can include meetings with both attorneys and the parties. In this option, the attorneys are typically only involved on the issues that the parties cannot resolve on their own. Since attorneys are not usually trained in mental health or financial planning, if there are complex emotional or financial issues, the parties must handle those issues themselves or hire additional professionals.

G. Hybrid Options

The time and cost of litigation or arbitration can be reduced by combining it with other options. For example, a mediator is sometimes brought in to assist with settling specific issues in a litigation case.

---

1. Supports and the Future, and Dealing with the Now

As anyone approaches a divorce, concerns are multifaceted. Consider a tree as an analogy. In order for it to thrive, all of its many branches have to be tended to be nourished. Attending to the legal issues alone results in a lopsided tree that will eventually pull itself from the soil and crash to the ground.

Our case example of Theresa and David's family restructuring exemplifies of how complex a divorce can be. While dealing with the pragmatics of relocating, and the multitude of details which moving entails, Theresa needed many supports--not least psychological and financial ones. The latter of these had to be intertwined with her choices about where and how to live.

We will use Theresa and David's restructuring to help guide you through your own restructuring.

Financial Planner: Anyone involved in a divorce will learn that considerations about support and settlements are important--but oftentimes parties neglect to plan how that support (spousal and child) and settlement will be deployed. While working through financial issues with a planner, Theresa had to evaluate which of the hundreds of personal and household items she and David acquired over twenty-two years of their living together Theresa wanted to keep.

Realtor: Decisions about the home are primary and emotionally charged. Does Theresa want to remain in the house? Will David want to? If they decide to sell, they'll need a realtor. Could she and David agree on a realtor? If so, Theresa knew she would be the person primarily responsible for engaging one.

There are many considerations when hiring a realtor: his or her track record, number of sales in the past year, current listings, personality, and commission fees, as well as whether their fees are negotiable. The realtor would help them determine if the house needs to be de-cluttered, painted, landscaped, or repaired--more details to be organized, more experts and household workers to be hired.

Therapist: While juggling the realities of a potential house sale and coming to understand possible financial outcomes, it was equally important for Theresa to attend to her mental health and that of her children. She hadn't been working with a therapist when we first met, so I recommended a few for her to meet with. I also wanted to help her create a list of therapists for her children, even though she didn't think they would immediately want to go to therapy.

When a client is not in therapy, I encourage him or her to gather names of therapists and begin interviewing them. It's important to find a therapist who has experience with grief and divorce. If, like Theresa, you are dealing with a particular issue such as sexuality, depression, or trauma, it's important to identify therapists with experience in those areas. Medical schools or hospitals in your area, as well as your pediatrician and school psychologist or social worker, are good places to start your search.

The American Psychological Association locator service (apa.org), also has lists of recommended therapists by location. Keep in mind that professionals pay to appear on lists, which are not usually vetted regarding particular experience and/or expertise. It's imperative that you prepare questions and interview several therapists before committing to one. Even if none of your children exhibits behavioral issues, those can erupt suddenly; having a therapist in mind alleviates the stress of needing to find someone compatible during a crisis mode.

Two roads diverged in a yellow wood,
And sorry I could not travel both
And be one traveler, long I stood
And looked down one as far as I could
To where it bent in the undergrowth;

Then took the other, as just as fair,
And having perhaps the better claim,
Because it was grassy and wanted wear;
Though as for that the passing there
Had worn them really about the same,

And both that morning equally lay
In leaves no step had trodden black.
Oh, I kept the first for another day!
Yet knowing how way leads on to way,
I doubted if I should ever come back.

I shall be telling this with a sigh
Somewhere ages and ages hence:
Two roads diverged in a wood, and I—
I took the one less travelled by,
And that has made all the difference.

-Robert Frost

Even if you are not the one who will be moving out of the family home, you will experience a profound shift in your social and perhaps even professional life.

Instead of beginning your divorce journey by filing a Complaint, giving little consideration to where that road will take you, we encourage you to employ the Consilium® Process of first asking yourself: "Where do I want to be in ten years?" Having a sense of where you want to be will change the nature of the journey upon which you are about to embark.

The second question we want you to ask yourself is, "How will I get there?"

You will need a roadmap detailing your goals and objectives regarding just about every aspect of your life. You should identify support systems and companions who will help you along this path. Although anyone who is divorcing will need to remain flexible and able to respond to shifting variables--the divorce is not about just one person, or even just two--having a goal and identifying benchmarks will go a long way toward getting you there. As someone wise once said, "Pessimists complain about the wind; optimists hope it will pick up; realists adjust the sails."

In planning your goals, imagine where you would like to be not just geographically, financially, and professionally, but also spiritually, socially, and family-wise. Visualize your restructured family as clearly as possible. Then, break your goals down into manageable time frames that can serve as benchmarks, such as one, three, and five years. Determining these factors will create the foundation upon which your decisions will rest.

Geographically, Theresa hoped to be living in both a Boston apartment and a Vermont home, both of which could accommodate all of her children. Professionally, she hoped to be running an art gallery. She wanted to preserve a civil relationship with David, so that the children could benefit from both of their parents' involvement in their lives. With that in mind, she hoped to work with David on an "after-marriage covenant"--an agreement detailing the joint aspirations and goals they held for their children. Socially, she hoped to engage with the gay community; spiritually, she planned to start yoga and meditation.

Having identified her long-term goals, Theresa was ready to begin the hard work of planning how to arrive at that lovely vision of the next phase in her and her family's lives.

In the workbook section of this book, you will find a goals section to get you started.

2. Financial health

Many impending divorcees worry about whether they will be able to remain in the family home; others have the luxury of also considering whether the family will be able to maintain an existing vacation home.

Oftentimes a family lives large, and accrues significant amounts of debt. In other cases, the reverse is true: couples have savings and monies that allow them latitude in their post-divorce lifestyle. In either case, it's important to have a clear picture of the family's debt situation, as the devil you know is always better than the devil you don't.

When people live beyond their means, it's important to understand that and make lifestyle adjustments as rapidly as possible, to ensure a smooth transition. Negotiated settlements can be made with creditors, but it's not a good idea to do so in the throes of a divorce. Such settlements can destroy one or both parties' credit, and compromise future purchasing abilities and lifestyle choices.

Working with a financial planner is essential, but on your own you can begin to identify the values of your assets, such as liquid assets, home, investments, retirement funds, life insurance policies, profit sharing, and annuities, as well as debts, including mortgages, loans, auto payments, and any other personal and/or business outstanding credit card debt.

The Financial section in the workbook section of this book will help you assess your family assets, debts, regular income, and expenses, as well as help you highlight likely challenges you might encounter regarding real estate decisions, and the education and mental health of you, your spouse, and your children. If you don't know how to complete some parts of the form, don't panic. At least you will have identified what you need to learn! Even that is a great step forward.

3. Health insurance

Many clients are concerned about their health insurance. A stay-at-home mom might be fortunate enough to have a family health insurance plan through her spouse's employer in which she and the children will continue to be eligible to participate. However, if that is not the case, it is an important factor to identify immediately. It's also important to understand that if one spouse has a health insurance benefit through his or her employment, and covers the other spouse through that plan, the non-employee's continuing coverage may be impacted if the employee spouse remarries.

The Health section of the workbook will help you evaluate the details of your health insurance plan, insurance agent, and other information. If you don't have a health insurance plan or agent, it is time to find someone who can help you sort through available choices.

What about disability, long-term care, and life insurance? If you aren't solidly familiar with your coverages, you should prioritize remedying that. If you will be receiving spousal and child support, it is important to know that in the event of your spouse's disability or death, you will continue to have a viable income stream. If you do not currently have adequate coverage, now is the time to secure insurance policies for such an eventuality. With your financial planner and insurance agent, determine target amounts necessary in case of disability or death. It's also prudent to determine whether you should add any long-term care insurance.

4. Mental Health

Again, it is ideal for you to interview and identify therapists for yourself and your children. Clarify what you most want to achieve in therapy. Are you looking to examine your personal history? Achieve goal-based outcomes moving forward? Some of each? Which are your priorities? How much time (and money) are you able and willing to devote to each process? Different therapies have different goals, philosophies, and training, and knowing your goals, will allow you to work toward vital outcomes.

Ask yourself--and answer honestly--whether you or your children are suffering acutely from, or are symptomatic of, any mental illness. Determine whether medication could be useful or is necessary. Only psychiatrists can prescribe medication. If you think behavioral or talk therapy will be most useful, a psychologist or licensed social worker may meet your goals. Some psychiatrists have clinical-based practices where they see patients for both talk therapy and medication.

In the Mental Health section of the workbook, complete the section on therapy goals for yourself and your children, and information on professionals to interview.

5. Script for talking with the children

One of the toughest parts of moving toward a divorce is talking to your children about what will be happening and the changes they will be experiencing. You should not approach this situation without a plan, and a script can be an extremely helpful starting point.

To create a script, you must consider the developmental stages and readiness of each of your children: those facts will determine what kind of information they can readily digest.

It is best if you and your spouse can talk to your children together, but sometimes that is not possible. Additionally, you will need to determine whether or not to tell multiple children together, or independently. Telling a six-year-old and a sixteen-year-old about their parents' plans to divorce will be two completely different conversations. Forethought, pre-writing, and even practicing your script is advisable. Working on it together is ideal.

Sometimes, one parent has specific personal information he or she would like to discuss with one or all of the children without the other parent's presence. As long as both parents understand why that is, and what will be said in their absence, this approach can be entirely appropriate. For instance, Theresa wanted to tell the children that although she'd been living a straight lifestyle for many years, she had realized that in order for her to live authentically, she needed to come out as gay. As David was struggling with his own feelings of betrayal, sadness, and anger, Theresa didn't want his emotions to dominate the message he delivered to their children. Despite the friction between them, David agreed that it was Theresa's message to share. She shared with David what she planned to say, and David agreed it was appropriate. They also agreed to tell their children separately, as they ranged in age from ten to eighteen, and they imagined each would react differently and need different information. They also agreed that about a week after each of them had separate conversations with their children, they would sit down and talk together as a group. They reasoned that the children would likely be a valuable source of support for one another and that any follow-up discussions about the separation and divorce could still be handled separately.

A sample script appears in the workbook section of this book.

6. Wills, Estates, and Guardianships

After your divorce, you will need to revise your Will and Estate plan or create one if you don't have one. Ideally, you and your spouse will be able to discuss and agree upon custody and guardianship provisions for your children in the event you were both to die during your children's minority. You may also want to revise health care proxies and powers of appointment.

PART VII: YOUR WORKBOOK OF PERSONAL GROWTH

If not now, when? - **Rabbi Hillel**

If you'd like to receive a printable version of this form please request it from us via email at TheConsiliumPath.com The subject line should read: Dissolution to Evolution Printable Form.

If you see your divorce not only as a fractured time but also as a point of growth, you will be better able to move forward effectively and empowered. The following questions are intended to help you think about where you've been and where you want to go.

1. What are you most passionate about in life? (e.g. personally, professionally, family)

2. What are you most afraid of happening after your divorce?

3. What are you most looking forward to post divorce?

4. If you look ahead 3 years from now, what would need to happen for you to feel satisfied about your decision to divorce?

5. What are your personal life goals? (e.g. educationally, career-wise, spiritually, physically?)

Year 1 -
Year 3 -
Year 5 -

The following questions are intended to help you reflect upon your marital history and patterns so that you can think through their likely impact on your abilities and those of your spouse to best move from the dissolution of your marriage to the evolution of your restructured family.

What will bring out your best and most generous tendencies, and those of your spouse? And what will bring out the worst in each of you? What will get your ire up, and what are the "buttons" you know will push your spouse? Which of the possible legal processes is most likely to help you not only through your divorce, but in your post divorce, restructured family life?

Marriage and Family History

1. Describe what attracted you to your spouse:

2. What do you think your spouse would say attracted him/her to you?

3. What irritates/angers you about your spouse?

4. What do you think irritates/angers your spouse about you?

5. What happens when you argue with your spouse? Does one person scream? Does the other scream back? Go silent? Walk away? Are problems resolved?

6. Briefly describe the family/household dynamic you grew up in. How has this affected the relationship you have with your spouse?

7. Describe the family/household dynamic your spouse grew up in. How do you believe this has affected the relationship he has with you?

8. Are there any other people or circumstances that have affected your marriage contributing to its current state? If so, describe them.

Children

Once you've reflected upon your children's personalities, and their unique relationships with you and your spouse, and any special needs they may have, you can include them in your planning and your decision as to how best tell them about your divorce.

No matter how old your children are when you and your spouse decide to divorce, the most important take-away message for your children will be that the decision the two of you have made has absolutely nothing to do with your love for them. Your decision to no longer be married to each other is in no way your children's fault.

1. List the names and ages of your children.

2. List a few words that best describe each of your children.

```
┌─────────────────────────────────────────────┐
│                                             │
├─────────────────────────────────────────────┤
│                                             │
├─────────────────────────────────────────────┤
│                                             │
├─────────────────────────────────────────────┤
│                                             │
├─────────────────────────────────────────────┤
│                                             │
├─────────────────────────────────────────────┤
│                                             │
├─────────────────────────────────────────────┤
│                                             │
└─────────────────────────────────────────────┘
```

3. List a few positive aspects of your relationship with your children:

```
┌─────────────────────────────────────────────┐
│                                             │
├─────────────────────────────────────────────┤
│                                             │
├─────────────────────────────────────────────┤
│                                             │
├─────────────────────────────────────────────┤
│                                             │
├─────────────────────────────────────────────┤
│                                             │
├─────────────────────────────────────────────┤
│                                             │
├─────────────────────────────────────────────┤
│                                             │
└─────────────────────────────────────────────┘
```

4. List a few negative aspects of your relationship with your children

```
_____
_____
_____
_____
_____
_____
_____
_____
```

5. List a few positive aspects of your spouse's relationship with your children.

```
_____
_____
_____
_____
_____
_____
_____
_____
```

6. List a few negative aspects of your spouse's relationship with your children.

```
_____
_____
_____
_____
_____
_____
_____
_____
```

7. If any of your children have educational, emotional and/or physical need or concerns, please describe them below.

```
_____
_____
_____
_____
_____
_____
_____
_____
```

Depending upon the ages of your children and their observations of your marriage and its discord, they will be more or less ready to hear about your decision to divorce. However, it is fair to say that all children will feel a sense of loss when their parents tell them that they are divorcing. Even in families where there is a lot of fighting and outright discord, children often hope that their parents will resolve their differences and remain married. That having been said, in many instances there is also a sense of relief that everyone in the family will feel. It is not unusual for children to thrive in many unexpected ways once their parents decide to separate. Your honesty often is a validation of their reality and makes everyone able to live an authentic life.

By creating a "script" neither of you will be surprised by what the other says, and together you will be better able to anticipate your children's concerns. By telling your children together, they will see that despite your decision to get divorced, you are able to work together and you will be able to support them as they grow. Your task is to move from being spouses to being co-parents, and by seeing yourselves as co-parents instead of ex-spouses, you and your children will be better able to envision a positive future.

When you create your script, you will want to provide your children with essential facts, but not get into any details as to the reasons for the divorce, other than to say that you both feel that you'd be happier not living together and would be able to be better parents to them if you were not married. Your children will worry about how your decision will impact them. Probable topics and concerns may be:

1. Where will we live?

2. Will we be selling our house?

3. Will I be changing schools?

4. Will I still be able to participate in sports/dance/music lessons, etc.?

5. Have you told my teacher/coach/extended family, etc.?

6. What will happen to our family pet?

7. How do I tell my friends?

8. Will we still go to church or temple together?

9. How will we celebrate holidays?

10. Who will I vacation with?

11. Will I still go to summer camp?

12. Do I still get an allowance? How will that work?

It's helpful for you to have discussed these things with each other before you talk to your children. You may not know the answers to many of these questions. If you don't know the answers to the questions they ask, it's important to let your children know that although you do not know the answers yet (e.g.- will you be selling your house, will they be changing schools), you will work together to let them know as soon as you do have answers. As best you can try to put yourself in their position and under-stand that although you are making decisions, you want them to feel that they have as much control as possible over whatever decisions they might be able to make. For instance, if you will be moving, will they get to choose the color of the paint in their new room? Anything you can realistically give them to hold on to will be helpful. It is also important that in advance of your conversation with your children, you and your spouse discuss the time frame for changes, such as when one person will be moving out of the house and when a shared parenting arrangement will begin. In order to provide the most security possible for your children, you and your spouse should literally take a calendar and identify known anticipated events. It is best not to tell your children you are divorcing until you have a plan and can tell them when changes will occur.

Difficult as it is to hear your children's concerns, it is important to allow them to ask questions, to feel sad, to cry, to express worries, concerns and fears. It is also important to allow them to imagine a time when things will have changed, when everyone is in a better place, and how you all as a family will work to make that happen.

(b) EXAMPLE SCRIPT

Parent A: There's something important Mom/Dad and I want to talk to you about.

Parent B: You know that your Mom/Dad and I love you both very, very much. Nothing in the world could ever change that.

Parent A: Just like you're not the same person you were when you were 3 (if you're now 9 for instance), Mom/Dad and I aren't the same people we were when we first met each other and fell in love. However, like Mom/Dad said one thing has never and could never change and that is how much we both love you.

Parent B: What has changed is our ability to make each other happy. We don't seem able to live together and bring out the best in each other anymore.

Parent A: Sometimes when people grow and change, they realize they would be happier if they no longer lived together.

Parent B: Mom/Dad and I have talked a lot and we've both decided it would be best for our family if we didn't live together anymore. Therefore, we've decided that I'll be moving to _____ on _____. It's about ___ miles from here. That's close enough so that you can spend good amounts of time with both of us and

Parent A: We can both get to your _____ (plays, sporting events, etc.) just as we always have.

Parent B: Do you have questions?

The first is likely to be "Are you getting divorced?" The answer is "yes, we are". Do not sugar coat or alter that answer if you are committed to your decision. If it's a trial separation you can say that but if you've decided to move forward to divorce do not say "we're not sure or we'll see as time goes on". Tearing off a bandaid is less painful than slowly pulling at every hair. Having discussed this in advance with each other, you will be prepared for their anger or sadness or relief.

Depending upon the ages of your children you may want to give them journals to record their questions and concerns so that they can think about everything over time and ask you questions later on.

(c) Finances

It is important for you to have a firm understanding of your family's finances. If your financial house is in disarray, it is important to address as many of those problems as you can before you divorce (e.g.- your credit score or an underwater mortgage).

Monthly Income (Gross)

Paycheck A (Gross)	$
FICA tax	$
State tax	$
Retirement Contributions	$
Income	$
Subtotal A	$

Paycheck B (Gross)	$
FICA tax	$
State tax	$
Retirement Contributions	$
Additional Income	$
Subtotal B	$

Total Income (Subtotal A + Subtotal B)	$

Monthly Expenses

Home

Mortgage/Rent	$
Gas/Oil	$
Water/Sewer	$
Electricity	$
Telephone (include cell phones)	$
Cable/Internet	$
Yard (plowing, landscaping etc.)	$
Home Equity Loan	$
Home Insurance	$
TOTAL	$

Car

Car Payment	$
Gas	$
Car Insurance	$
Maintenance	$
TOTAL	$

Children

Day Care	$
After School Activities	$
Tutoring	$
Summer Camp	$
School Tuition	$
College Savings	$
TOTAL	$

Health

Insurance Premiums	$
Out-of-Pocket Medical Expenses	$
TOTAL	$

Miscellaneous

Groceries	$
Entertainment (movies, dining out, etc.)	$
Clothing	$
Vacation	$
Commuting (parking, etc.)	$
Life Insurance	$
Long Term Care Insurance	$
Retirement (IRA, etc.)	$
Emergency Fund	$
Charitable Contributions	$
Other -	$
Other -	$
Other -	$
TOTAL	$

Total Expenses

Total Home	$
Total Car	$
Total Children	$
Total Health	$
Total Miscellaneous	$
Total Expenses	$

Grand Totals

Total Income (Paycheck A + Paycheck B)	$
Total Expenses	$
Income Minus Expenses	$

It's important to clarify how, post-divorce, you will exchange pertinent information and documents that provide you with financial security (e.g.- income tax returns (if spousal and/or child support might be impacted through changes in salary and bonuses), life, long-term care and disability insurance.

(d) The Law and the Courts

What the law and the Courts __can__ provide:

This list is not exhaustive, but it does include the most common things a client seeks.

- Spousal support

- Child support

- Child custody and child sharing

- Division of marital assets

- Division of marital debt

- The treatment of inherited money

- Health insurance

- Restraining orders

- Freezing of marital assets

- Disclosure of marital assets

- Maintenance of life insurance

- Orders for psychiatric, alcohol and drug related evaluations

- Orders for evaluation by guardians ad litem (lawyers or therapists appointed by the Court to represent the children's best interests, or to evaluate the dynamics of the family

Itemize what you think you need that the Court can provide for you. We suggest you fill out the grid below and take it to your lawyer and discuss with him/her the law of your specific state and what he/she thinks are achievable results based upon what you've determined you need.

1. _____
2. _____
3. _____
4. _____
5. _____

What the law and the Courts **cannot** provide:

- Punishment of your spouse
- Moral judgments
- Psychotherapy for you, your spouse or your children
- Vindication
- Healing
- Medication
- Education or further training
- Healthy eating habits
- Exercise
- Government assistance
- Friends
- Family
- Forgiveness

Itemize what you think you need that the Court cannot provide and ask yourself, who can provide the other things I need or crave? A therapist? A financial planner? Clergy? A personal trainer? Government assistance? Education? Retraining? Recreation? Friends? Family?

1. _____
2. _____
3. _____
4. _____
5. _____

Now that you have an understanding of what the Courts can and cannot provide, what are your top 3 goals for your divorce?

1. _____
2. _____
3. _____

What do you think your spouse's top 3 goals for your divorce are?

1. _____
2. _____
3. _____

Start thinking about what you have in common and what may be difficult to negotiate. Will you need help from a third party, like a financial advisor or therapist? Are there areas that you can both can agree upon from the start that will not need to be negotiated? Understanding what you want to accomplish will keep you focused on the most important aspects of your divorce while avoiding the emotions that will side track you.

Buddhist thought worth remembering…

**Refusing to forgive someone is like drinking poison
and expecting the other person to die.**

(e) Estate and Financial Planning

If you already have an estate plan with your spouse, it is important to update it after your divorce. The same is true for your financial plans. Answer the questions below to help you discover what you may need:

1. Do you currently have a financial planner? If yes, is this person shared by your spouse? If so, you will want to have separate planners post divorce. Will you have assets post divorce that will need to be managed by a professional portfolio manager? If yes, you will want to identify people to interview for that role. If you will instead need a financial plan post-divorce, you will want to interview fee for service planners who can help you create a plan.

2. Do you have a will? If yes, would you like to change any beneficiaries, executors, or guardianship of children? If no, what will happen with your assets/children if you predecease them?

3. Do you have a Power of Attorney? If yes, would you like to change any agents? If no, do you need to select people to assist you in the event you become sick or incapacitated?

4. Do you have a healthcare proxy? If yes, would you like to change it? If no, who will make your healthcare decisions if you are unable to speak for yourself?

5. Are you the donor of a Trust? If yes, would you like to change it?

6. Do you or your spouse expect to be the beneficiary of a Trust/Will? If so, this is something you need to address now as it may be a factor in your marital asset division.

(f) Educational and Mental Health Supports

Education

If your children have special needs it's important to try to clarify and identify them as best you can. Answer these questions for each of your children, and use additional paper if necessary.

1. Are any of your children on an Individualized Educational Plan (IEP)? If so, please list the circumstances and accommodations. Do any of your children need a neuropsychological evaluation to better assess their needs?

2. Do you suspect or has it been suggested to you that any of your children may have ADHD (inattentive or hyperactive), dyslexia, or be on the autism spectrum? Early diagnosis will lead you to early intervention, help, and a lifetime of success for your child. If you suspect such a diagnosis, identify to whom and where you'd like to go for help.

3. Do any of your children need extra support (academic or social-emotional)? If so, list your ideas as to where you can get the help that you need.

4. How will you and your spouse share the cost for any educational supports needed for your children? How long can you expect your children will need these services? Have you considered establishing a special fund or a Trust for these costs if you expect they might be needed for many years?

_____

5. Are you concerned that any of your children will not be able to live independently as adults? If so, please describe any planning you and your spouse have done for that time, including setting up a Special Needs Trust, investigating disabled adult housing and providing life insurance.

_____

(h) Psychological Needs

When looking for emotional support and psychological assistance, many resources are available to you. However, it's important to recognize that if you're looking for someone who can help you with the inevitable adjustments you're currently confronting, or other persistent psychological concerns, thinking ahead will help you better plan for the long-term good of your restructured family.

Ask yourself:

- Am I looking for someone who can help me talk through my current experience?
- If you're depressed, is the therapist experienced in depression? Grief and grieving? Can they prescribe anti-depressants (only psychiatrists and in some jurisdictions psychiatric social workers or psychiatric nurse practitioners can). If not, does the therapist you want to work with work in conjunction with someone who can prescribe medication?
- Is a licensed social worker, a psychologist or a psychiatrist the type of professional you want to work with?
- Are you looking for someone who can help you with a mood or anxiety disorder? Something you're struggling with now, but may also have been a consistent problem for you throughout your lifetime?
- Are you dealing with a high conflict personality, either your own or that of your spouse and want to better understand how to de-escalate your interactions?
- Are you looking for someone who is a couples therapist, and who could work with you and your spouse whether you remain together or not?
- Are you looking for a therapist who specializes in working with couples, affairs and betrayal?
- Are you looking for a family therapist?
- Are you looking for a child psychiatrist?
- Are you in need of an addiction specialist? (alcohol, drugs, gambling, sex - specialists exist in all these areas)

- Are you looking for help with obsessive compulsive disorders (OCD), sometimes manifested in hoarding behaviors?
- Are you looking for help with, or to better understand personality disorders (narcissism, antisocial, borderline, bipolar, paranoid or histrionic)?
- Are you looking for help with eating disorders or substance abuse?

Note that although a psychiatrist's fees will be more than those of a social worker, if it is likely that medication will be helpful, it is important to assess with a psychiatrist that component of treatment. You may want to see a psychiatrist only for a pharmacological consultation, and then continue in therapy with someone else. However, without a proper medical assessment, years could be misspent when they need not be.

We devised a short quiz to help you distill the option(s) that might be best for you to resolve your disagreements. The quiz is meant to be a guide, not an answer, as without having a fuller understanding of your unique circumstances, no quiz can give you a definitive plan.

QUIZ

Question 1: Privacy

Would you prefer that this dispute stay private?

Yes, I want to keep my privacy.
No, I want to expose the injustice of my situation.

Scoring: Yes= 3 No=0 _____

Question 2: Cost

How important is it to you that the resolution process be cost-effective?

Very Important

Important

Somewhat Important

Not Important

I Don't Know

Very Important = 10 = Important= 8, Somewhat Important & IDK = 5, Not Important = 0

Scoring: _____

Question 3: Time v. Control

How quickly do you want to settle your dispute?

A. As fast as possible.

B. Fast, but I don't want to just give in to get it done.

C. As long as it takes to get it right.

D. I want to drag this out as long as possible.

Scoring: A = 8, B = 9, C = 10, D =0_____

Question 4: Risk Averse (Control of Outcome)

You're at the casino and have $100, do you:

A. play poker

B. play blackjack

C. play roulette

D. play slot machine, or

E. go to a show or dinner.

Scoring: A = 6, B = 3 , C = 1, D = 0 , E = 8 _____

Question 5: Relationship

Do you care how your spouse thinks about you when this is over?

A. Their opinion is important to me.

B. I'd like to keep a civil relationship.

C. I don't care.

Scoring: A = 8, B = 7, C = 0 _____

Question 6: Trust

Do you believe your spouse will be truthful throughout the process?

A. Yes, I think being transparent is important to both of us.

B. I don't know if they will tell the truth.

C. I'm nervous they might lie because of how much is at stake.

D. I expect them to lie because they've lied to me before.

Scoring: A = 10, B = 5, C = 5, D = 0 _____

Question 7: Relationship

How often do you expect to see or communicate with your spouse after the dispute ends?

Very Often

Often

Sometimes

Never

I Don't Know

Very Often = 10, Often = 8, Sometimes = 7, Never = 0, IDK = 2

Scoring: _____

Question 8: Protections

Do you need protection from your spouse?

    A. No, I'm not concerned.

    B. I'm not sure.

    C. There are immediate issues to address but I think they will be resolvable.

    D. I am certain that immediate action is necessary in court to protect my interests and me.

    E. I am afraid of my spouse, as s/he is violent.

Scoring: A = 8, B = 10, C = 8, D = -40, E = -50 _____

Question 9: Privacy

How important is it to protect your privacy?

    Very Important

    Important

    Somewhat Important

    Not Important

I Don't Know

Very Important = 9, Important = 7, Somewhat Important =5, Not Important =3 IDK= 0

Scoring: _____

Question 10: Communication

Have you tried to discuss your disagreements with your spouse?

A. Yes, and we made some progress.

B. Yes, but we didn't get anywhere.

C. No, but I plan to do that.

D. No, I can't stand to speak to him/her.

Scoring: A = 9, B = 7, C = 6, D = 4 _____

Question 11: Complexity

Will you need additional experts to help you with some part of the dispute (e.g. appraisals, valuations, accounting, evaluations, etc.)?

A. Yes, the issues are very complex.

B. No, but the other side might think so.

C. I don't know.

D. No, this is a simple matter.

Scoring: A = 10, B = 9, C = 7, D = 6 _____

For Scores over 91 a good choice for you is likely to be:

Collaborative Law is the highest rated dispute resolution option based on your responses. Other option you have for resolving your dispute are: Mediation, Attorney Negotiation, Arbitration, Litigation.

For Scores between 82 and 90 a good choice for you is likely to be:

Collaborative Law and Mediation are the highest rated dispute resolution options based on your responses. Other option you have for resolving your dispute are: Attorney Negotiation, Arbitration, Litigation.

For Scores between 76 and 82 a good choice for you is likely to be:

Mediation is the highest rated dispute resolution option based on your responses. Other option you have for resolving your dispute are: Collaborative Law, Attorney Negotiation, Arbitration, Litigation.

For Scores between 67 and 82 a good choice for you is likely to be:

Mediation and Attorney Negotiation are the highest rated dispute resolution options based on your responses. Other option you have for resolving your dispute are: Collaborative Law, Arbitration, Litigation.

For Scores between 67 and 76 a good choice for you is likely to be:

Attorney Negotiation is the highest rated dispute resolution option based on your responses. Other option you have for resolving your dispute are: Collaborative Law, Mediation, Arbitration, Litigation.

For Scores between 57 and 76 a good choice for you is likely to be:

Attorney Negotiation and Arbitration are the highest rated dispute resolution options based on your responses. Other option you have for resolving your dispute are: Collaborative Law, Mediation, Litigation.

For Scores between 57 and 67 a good choice for you is likely to be:

Arbitration is the highest rated dispute resolution option based on your responses. Other option you have for resolving your dispute are: Collaborative Law, Mediation, Attorney Negotiation, Litigation.

For Scores between 51 and 56 a good choice for you is likely to be:

Arbitration and Litigation are the highest rated dispute resolution options based on your responses. Other option you have for resolving your dispute are: Collaborative Law, Mediation, Attorney Negotiation.

For Scores of 50 or below:

Litigation is the highest rated dispute resolution option based on your responses. Other options you have for resolving your dispute are: Collaborative Law, Attorney Assisted Mediation, Attorney Negotiation, Arbitration.

Intensity- A question to think about but not to score.

What movie most reminds you of your current situation?

A. It's Complicated
B. Psycho
C. War of the Roses
D. The Hangover
E. Kramer vs. Kramer

Would thinking about your situation as a different kind of movie alter your perspective and/or your goals? If the answer is yes and the outcome is more positive for you when you change it, write down for yourself what changes you made to improve your own perspective and your potential outcome.

_____

_____

_____

If you'd like to discuss your situation with a Conflict Assessment & Resolution professional, you may contact Consilium® Divorce Consultations (info@Consilium® divorce.com) directly.

GLOSSARY

Although not all of the words in this glossary are used in this book I've included them here as they are the "language of divorce", and understanding them will make the Family Court landscape more comprehensible.

A

Action: A lawsuit taken to court.

Adultery: Adultery is any sexual act, or deviate sexual act (as defined in the Penal Code), with another person at a time when that person has a living spouse. It has long been a cause for divorce but is not often claimed any longer.

Agreement: A formal written understanding between two people concerning their respective rights and their duties to each other.

Alternative Dispute Resolution: (ADR) refers to a variety of processes that help parties resolve disputes without a trial. Typical ADR processes include mediation, arbitration, neutral evaluation, and Collaborative Law. These processes are generally confidential, less formal, and often less stressful than traditional court proceedings.

Attorney for Child: An attorney appointed by the court to represent a child in contested custody matters.

C

Child Support: Money paid by one parent to another for a child's expenses after separation and/or divorce.

Cohabit: To live with, and usually have sexual relations with, another person.

Collaborative Law: Process in which couples hire specially-trained lawyers and other professionals who work to help them resolve their conflict out of court.

Commingle: When one mixes separate funds or properties into a common fund or bank account.

Contempt: The willful disregard and disrespect of a court order of the judge's authority. Conduct that defies the authority or dignity of a court. It is usually punishable by fine or prison or both.

Contested Divorce: A divorce action which is opposed.

Custody, Legal: The legal right to make major decisions affecting a child under the age of 18.

Custody, Physical: The actual physical care and control of a child under the age of 18. The person with physical custody usually provides the child's primary residence.

D

Defendant: The person against whom the divorce action is brought.

Deposition: A person's out-of-court, sworn testimony that is reduced to writing (usually by a court reporter) for later use in the lawsuit. Except for a judge not being present, it is conducted in a manner similar to trial. Also known as an Examination Before Trial (EBT)

Discovery: Required disclosure, at a party's request, of information that relates to the litigation. In divorce cases, it usually relates to financial information.

Divorce: The legal ending of the marriage between a husband and wife so that each is free to marry again.

E

Earning Capacity: A person's ability or power to earn money, given the person's talent, skills, training and experience

Egregious: Extremely or remarkably bad; shocking.

Emancipation: The release of a child from the responsibility and control of a parent or guardian. Also, usually the end of a financial obligation of support.

Equal Distribution: A means of dividing marital property as 50% of one asset to one party and 50% to the other. Some states are "equal division" states and some are "equitable division" states.

Equitable Distribution: A means of dividing marital property that does not necessarily mean 50% of one asset to one party and 50% to the other. Distribution is based on various factors presented to the court. Some states are "equitable division" states and some are "equal division" states.

Ex Parte (Communication): An application or statement made to the court by one party (including counsel) to a proceeding without notice to, or in the absence of, the other party.

Expert: A person who, through education or experience, has developed skills or knowledge of a particular subject, so that he or she may form an opinion that will assist the judge or jury in making a decision.

F

Fault-Based Divorce: divorce action where misconduct by one spouse is needed before a marriage may be ended.

Fault Grounds: marital misconduct giving one spouse a legal reason to sue for divorce, such as abuse, abandonment or adultery.

Fiduciary: One who must use a high standard of care in managing another's money or property.

Filing: Giving the clerk of Court your legal papers.

G

Grounds for Divorce: the legal basis for a divorce; the law sets out specific reasons for a divorce which have to be proven before the court can grant a divorce.

Guardian ad litem: A guardian, usually a lawyer, appointed by the court to help a minor or incompetent person in a lawsuit. In a divorce case, the guardian ad litem does not act as an attorney for the child, but reports to the court on what is in the child's best interests.

I

Interrogatory: A written question or a set of questions given to the other party in a lawsuit as part of discovery.

Irreconcilable Differences: In some states this is legal ground for a no-fault divorce.

Irretrievable Breakdown: In some states this is a legal ground for a no-fault divorce.

J

Judgment of Divorce: A document signed by the court granting the divorce.

Jurisdiction: The authority of the court to hear a case.

L

Legal Separation: a court order allowing spouses to live separate and apart while remaining legally married.

M

Marital Property: Any property, regardless of which person is named as owner, that the parties obtained from the date of marriage to the beginning of the divorce action. A house, car, IRA, bank account(s), pension, annuity, business and advanced degree are all examples of marital property. However, some property such as an inheritance, a gift from someone other than your spouse, or compensation for personal injuries, may be deemed separate property.

Mediation: A neutral person called a "mediator" helps the parties try to reach a mutually-acceptable resolution of their disputes. The mediator does not decide the case, but helps the parties communicate so they can try to settle their disagreements without other intervention. Mediation may be inappropriate if a party has a significant advantage in power or control over the other.

N

Non-Custodial Parent: a parent who does not have physical custody of the parties' child or children.

O

Order: A direction of the court. Failure to comply may result in contempt. (See Contempt)

P

Party: A Plaintiff or Defendant in a legal proceeding.

Plaintiff: The person who begins the divorce action/lawsuit.

Prenuptial Agreement: a contract signed by the spouses before the before the marriage setting out each spouse's rights to property and assets in the case of a divorce.

Postnuptial Agreement: a contract signed by the spouses after their marriage setting out each spouse's rights to property and assets in the case of a divorce.

Pro Se: (Self-Represented) Appearing on one's own behalf without an attorney.

Q

Qualified Domestic Relations Order (QDRO): a Court Order giving one spouse a share of the other spouse's pension or retirement funds.

S

Separate Property: Property considered by the courts to belong only to one spouse or the other.

Separation/ Settlement Agreement: A formal, voluntary, written agreement on all of the issues surrounding divorce. It must be formally signed and acknowledged by a Notary Public in order to be allowed and enforceable by the Court.

Spouse: Husband or wife.

Stipulation: A voluntary agreement between parties on an issue or issues related to the divorce proceedings.

Subpoena: A legal order requiring a person's attendance at a particular time and place to testify as a witness or to provide certain documents that are requested. Failure to comply can be contempt of court.

Support: Payment for housing, food, clothing, and related living expenses.

T

Temporary Support: payments made by one spouse to the other for financial support while the divorce action is pending.

U

Unemancipated Children: Children who are supported by a parent or guardian. (See Emancipation)

Uncontested Divorce: An uncontested divorce occurs when: (a) there are no disagreements between you and your spouse over any financial or divorce-related issues (i.e., child custody and support, division of marital property or spousal support); and (b) your spouse either agrees to the divorce, or fails to appear in the divorce action.

V

Venue: The permissible place for the trial of a lawsuit.